PERSONAL, ACCESSIBLE, RESPONSIVE, STRATEGIC

RESOURCES AND STRATEGIES FOR ONLINE WRITING INSTRUCTORS

PRACTICES & POSSIBILITIES

Series Editors: Nick Carbone and Mike Palmquist

Series Associate Editors: Karen-Elizabeth Moroski and Aleashia Walton

The Practices & Possibilities Series addresses the full range of practices within the field of Writing Studies, including teaching, learning, research, and theory. From Joseph Williams' reflections on problems to Richard E. Young's taxonomy of "small genres" to Adam Mackie's considerations of technology, the books in this series explore issues and ideas of interest to writers, teachers, researchers, and theorists who share an interest in improving existing practices and exploring new possibilities. The series includes both original and republished books. Works in the series are organized topically.

The WAC Clearinghouse, Colorado State University Open Press, and University Press of Colorado are collaborating so that these books will be widely available through free digital distribution and low-cost print editions. The publishers and the series editors are committed to the principle that knowledge should freely circulate. We see the opportunities that new technologies have for further democratizing knowledge. And we see that to share the power of writing is to share the means for all to articulate their needs, interest, and learning into the great experiment of literacy.

OTHER BOOKS IN THE SERIES

Cheryl Geisler & Jason Swarts, Coding *Streams of Language: Techniques for the Systematic Coding of Text, Talk, and Other Verbal Data* (2019)

Ellen C. Carillo, *A Guide to Mindful Reading* (2017)

Lillian Craton, Renée Love & Sean Barnette (Eds.), *Writing Pathways to Student Success* (2017)

Charles Bazerman, *Involved: Writing for College, Writing for Your Self* (2015)

Adam Mackie, *New Literacies Dictionary: Primer for the Twenty-first Century Learner* (2011)

Patricia A. Dunn, *Learning Re-abled: The Learning Disability Controversy and Composition Studies* (2011)

Richard E. Young, *Toward A Taxonomy of "Small" Genres and Writing Techniques for Writing Across the Curriculum* (2011)

Joseph M. Williams, *Problems into PROBLEMS: A Rhetoric of Motivation* (2011)

Charles Bazerman, *The Informed Writer: Using Sources in the Disciplines* (2011)

PERSONAL, ACCESSIBLE, RESPONSIVE, STRATEGIC

RESOURCES AND STRATEGIES FOR ONLINE WRITING INSTRUCTORS

By Jessie Borgman and Casey McArdle

The WAC Clearinghouse
wac.colostate.edu
Fort Collins, Colorado

University Press of Colorado
upcolorado.com
Louisville, Colorado

The WAC Clearinghouse, Fort Collins, Colorado 80523–1040

University Press of Colorado, Louisville, Colorado 80027

ISBN 978-1-64215-032-2 (PDF) | 978-1-64215-033-9 (ePub) | 978-1-60732-981-7 (pbk.)

Printed in the United States of America

Library of Congress Cataloging-in-Publication Data

Names: Borgman, Jessie, 1980– author. | McArdle, Casey, 1974– author.
Title: Personal, accessible, responsive, strategic : resources and strategies for online writing instructors / by Jessie Borgman and Casey McArdle.
Description: Fort Collins, Colorado : The WAC Clearinghouse ; Louisville, Colorado : University Press of Colorado, [2019] | Series: Practices & possibilities | Includes bibliographical references. | Summary: "By focusing on being Personal, Accessible, Responsive, and Strategic (PARS), this book explores the complexities and anxieties associated with Online Writing Instruction (OWI). The book offers examples of how to create personal assignments, syllabi, and learning spaces that connect with students while teaching instructors how to be accessible and craft accessible documents and spaces. The authors argue that when instructors create an online writing course, they are crafting a user experience and that, by borrowing from user experience practices, they encourage instructors to be strategic in planning and teaching their online courses"— Provided by publisher.
Identifiers: LCCN 2019045352 (print) | LCCN 2019045353 (ebook) | ISBN 9781607329817 (paper back) | ISBN 9781642150322 (pdf) | ISBN 9781642150339 (epub)
Subjects: LCSH: English language—Composition and exercises—Web-based instruction.
Classification: LCC PE1404 .B665 2019 (print) | LCC PE1404 (ebook) | DDC 808.02—dc23
LC record available at https://lccn.loc.gov/2019045352
LC ebook record available at https://lccn.loc.gov/2019045353

Copyeditor: Don Donahue
Designer: Mike Palmquist
Cover and Interior Photos: Courtesy of Jessie Borgman and Casey McArdle
Series Editors: Nick Carbone and Mike Palmquist
Series Associate Editors: Karen-Elizabeth Moroski and Aleashia Walton

The WAC Clearinghouse supports teachers of writing across the disciplines. Hosted by Colorado State University, and supported by the Colorado State University Open Press, it brings together scholarly journals and book series as well as resources for teachers who use writing in their courses. This book is available in digital formats for free download at wac.colostate.edu.

Founded in 1965, the University Press of Colorado is a nonprofit cooperative publishing enterprise supported, in part, by Adams State University, Colorado State University, Fort Lewis College, Metropolitan State University of Denver, Regis University, University of Colorado, University of Northern Colorado, Utah State University, and Western Colorado University. For more information, visit upcolorado.com.

Contents

Foreword

Scott Warnock
DREXEL UNIVERSITY

I've worked with Casey and Jessie for years in organizations and roles connected with online writing instruction and online literacy instruction (OWI and OLI). They work hard. They are creative. They have good spirits. They are *doers*. Through The Online Writing Instruction Community site, they have built, well, a community of instructors interested in OWI: Just what it says it is. *The PARS (Personal, Accessible, Responsive, Strategic) Approach to Online Writing Instruction* continues that mission. In *The PARS Approach,* they have set up a method of OWI that is lively and usable and encourages teachers to take on OWI and *do* it.

In the book, Jessie and Casey make a commitment to a *version* of teaching. They use golf (and all of its terminology) as a metaphor throughout the book to frame and illustrate their version of teaching and the PARS approach. They say, "the goal of our text is to offer one specific approach to OWI, the PARS approach," and that is indeed what they do. Materials about OWI are often broad, in a perhaps well-meaning effort to appeal to a wide range of teachers and pedagogies. That is fine, but Casey and Jessie say, "Up until this point, there has not been a book written with one distinct approach to OWI." This overt specificity is a strength of their book: In what follows you will find a *method*, a way to teach, that while it's based on generally good teaching theory, is also quite usable.

I think almost all teachers will find here a teaching piece specifically for their class[rooms], and for some instructors, particular the many contingent faculty who Jessie and Casey say "are often relied upon to teach online writing courses more frequently than full-time or tenured faculty," this book can offer a comprehensive approach. PARS can help when there is little training for these faculty, which is unfortunately too often the case. Many schools, the authors say, offer these teachers "little to no training," and while these faculty, "due to their resilience," often still do a good job, "this happens with more extra work and headaches than would occur were professional development support made available."

The authors write with poise and confidence. They say, "When instructors combine the four elements of the PARS approach, being an online writing instructor can seem more manageable." Why shouldn't they be confident? They are experienced teachers, and their stories of teaching run throughout the book. Interestingly, they both started out, as many of you no doubt have or will, as hybrid instructors. They also say, "We've self-taught ourselves one too many times on basic skills and strategies," and they hope their book helps you avoid that.

As teachers, they are student-centered in ways specific to OWI: Online *and* writing courses. For example, they recognize that particularly when teaching online, instructor connection with students takes time: "It takes strategy and time to show your students how much you care about them." They also point out how trust is built in the specific context of writing instruction: "Students need to build a relationship of trust with you as their instructor because they are sharing something very personal with you: their writing."

In fact, the strength of this book is that the approach they describe is highly practical, down to day-to-day activities. They raise topics like how to re-think how you handle email when you teach online. They offer advice about finding out, on the front end, what hardware you will need. They discuss scheduling and time, which are challenges for teachers and students in online instructional settings. In a good representation of their voice, they write: "Create a schedule that works for you and stick to it!"

This practical guidance stretches across all four PARS components. For instance, in terms of (p)ersonal, they say they "have inviting personalities" and they "encourage students through multiple means to interact" with them, while pointing out that "[i]nstructing students from a distance requires more work on the instructor's part. It challenges instructors to be their best self in every mode of communication and that's hard!" Jessie offers a personal bio as an example. Responsive is a key aspect of OWI, and they describe numerous strategies while making clear that "Responsive is different than being available." PARS is all about (s)trategic: being strategic "is a pillar to success in distance education. The most important thing a (novice or experienced) instructor or administrator can do is be [W1] strategic about their process." In being strategic, they circle back to the students: "We tend to apply user-centered practices . . . "

Finally, accessibility has been a central idea for those working in OWI. It was Principle 1 in the 2013 CCCC "A Position Statement of Principles and Example Effective Practices for Online Writing Instruction (OWI)" and remains first in the newly released Global Society of Online Literacy Educators' "Online Literacy Instruction Principles and Tenets." Casey and Jessie have locked onto OWI as an (a)ccessible practice, whether that accessibility is codified or not: "While this principle is not explicit in terms of meeting ADA guidelines, we believe that if you build your materials from the ground up with accessibility in mind, you will create a learning environment that is more inclusive than any other." They also make sure accessibility encompasses not just the courses, but the administration of them: for online writing program administrators (OWPAs), "being accessible for your colleagues is an essential part of administration." Sometimes, in the hustle and bustle of not just our terms but our professional lives, we forget that hype aside, online learning is still accompanied by tremendous promise. Jessie and Casey reinforce this, saying that distance education has "brought education to those that may have never even dreamed of a college degree." But if the courses are not accessible, not just to students but those who teach and administer, the education will never reach its potential.

Look, my knowledge of OWI definitely surpasses my knowledge of golf. I have only played a handful of times (not counting mini-golf), and those few rounds mostly ended because I had run out of golf balls: The ones I had were nestled in the woods, across some road, or at the bottom of a pond. In South Carolina, during a round I played in college, my friend's father grew exasperated, especially as I tried to fish a *slightly* mis-hit ball out of the water. "You're going to get eaten by an alligator!" he finally yelled, wondering why he had paid for me.

So I'm a great audience, because despite my minimal golf knowledge, the metaphor that drives the book spoke to me. "Golf is a great game for novices to learn," Casey and Jessie say: "[. . .] people hopefully enjoy the game for what it is—a game against yourself." They emphasize that "with practice everyone gets better," and they use that concept to build the connection to OWI, OWI administration, and course design. "When we play (teach, administer or design an OWI course) and get small 'wins,'" they write, "we want to keep going and make ourselves better. When we golf, and when we teach writing in an online setting, we aim to be 'par for the course' (pun intended), so the acronym is a good fit, albeit a little cheesy." They self-deprecatingly (that's what academics love to do!) say their acronym is a "little cheesy," but I think it fits with what they try to accomplish. (Note I have resisted the urge to have a play on words with golf and "*Fore*word." Now I've done it—there's *apophasis* for all you rhetoricians out there!)

In line with its overall practical bent, *The PARS Approach* helps them describe a tangible way of approaching virtual teaching. "For the hole in one!" sections are pointed and helpful, such as the advice to use icebreakers. The "Drive for Show, Putt for Dough!" sidebars provide discussion of "relevant activities or strategies" that they use in their "own individual online writing courses." Using PARS also clearly helped them compose in an accessible writing style, and, again, one that is filled with teaching stories—we need more stories of teaching! You are not reading a lecture from two out-of-touch noodlers. No, they have been doing the work of OWI. I think you will be able to relate to them.

They open and close with the statement that "we're all online writing instructors." I agree (Hewett & Warnock, 2015). As they point out, the logistics of instruction and the culture of writing involve digital tools in increasing ways now. But there is also a distinct group of those interested in OWI. In the broader field of composition and rhetoric, OWI carved out a robust and *caring* place for people with similar interests to meet and work. At conferences, particularly at the annual CCCC meeting (which is where I met both Jessie and Casey), OWI teachers, administrators, and scholars would come together, eager not only to share ideas and research, but for fellowship. This may be particularly important in OWI, as Casey and Jessie say: "Those without a home institution or those stringing together work at multiple institutions especially benefit from instructor to instructor camaraderie." As they note, I was hoping even back in 2009 for a digital community space for online writing instructors "so as to maximize the best practices of instruction and to refine our own approaches" (Hewett & Warnock, 2015, p. 166).

In that saying, I was in some way beckoning to Stephen North's articulation of the composition "House of lore," a lovely metaphor of writing instructional knowledge, a structure he describes as "a rambling, to my mind delightful old manse" (North, 1987, p. 27). The "House of lore" has always appealed to me, as I see the fundamental truth of it. All of our teaching knowledge is stored in the collective mind of composition teachers, but it is dispersed: How do we share it? How do we catalogue and disseminate the vast knowledge about teaching and our field in general that is being created every day?

This book does its part. *The PARS Approach* will help you *not* start from scratch. Jessie and Casey provide you with a usable framework to make OWI less burdensome. At the end, they say: "We hope that through reading the chapters in this text you feel better equipped to plan for and mitigate those friction points in your online writing courses." Let me follow their golf metaphor: This book will help you avoid many teaching sand traps, but the authors also recognize that you are going to land in one now and again, so it also provides you with ways and strategies to wedge your way out (look at me, communicating in golf-speak!). In OWI and composition in general, we need more experts sharing practices and more metaphors for such instruction. In the pages that follow is a way to that sharing, and an approach, a method, that I think will appeal to many of you.

References

Hewett, B. L. & Warnock, S. (2015). The future of OWI. In B. L. Hewett & K. DePew (Eds.), *Foundational practices of online writing instruction* (pp. 553–569). Fort Collins, CO: The WAC Clearinghouse and Parlor Press. Retrieved from https://wac.colostate.edu/books/perspectives/owi/

North, S. M. (1987). *The Making of knowledge in composition: Portrait of an emerging field.* Portsmouth, NH: Boynton/Cook Heinemann.

Warnock, S. (2009). *Teaching writing online: How and why.* Urbana, IL: NCTE.

Abbreviations and Key Terms

Agile = Agile software development describes a set of principles for software development under which requirements and solutions evolve through the collaborative effort of self-organizing cross-functional teams.

Admin. = administrator

CMS = Content Management System

F2F or f2f = face-to-face as in face-to-face classes or instruction

LMS = Learning Management System

Instructor/Teacher = used interchangeably to indicate someone who teaches writing

MSU = Michigan State University (where Casey works)

19th Hole = In golf, the nineteenth hole is a slang term for a pub, bar, or restaurant on or near the golf course, very often the clubhouse itself. A standard round of golf only has 18 holes.

UCD = user-centered design

UX = user experience

OLI = online literacy instruction

OWC = online writing course

OWI = online writing instruction or online writing instructor (used interchangeably)

OWIC = The Online Writing Instruction Community (our website)

OWPA = online writing program administrator

PARS = personal, accessible, responsive, strategic

Par = "par" stands for the number of strokes a golfer is expected to take on a particular hole; it's the score a scratch golfer with a zero handicap (i.e., a really good player) would expect to make.

ROI = return on investment

VOC =voice of customer

PERSONAL, ACCESSIBLE, RESPONSIVE, STRATEGIC

RESOURCES AND STRATEGIES FOR ONLINE WRITING INSTRUCTORS

Introduction:
Reflectiveness Paves the Way for Action

This book is about online writing instruction (OWI), community and access. Like others that have come before us, we argue that due to the digital nature of writing in this day and age, **we're all online writing instructors** (we even made T-Shirts to reiterate this!). We say and believe this because we know that so many face-to-face (F2F) writing classes are pretty much hybrid or blended writing courses given their use of digital spaces (for turning in assignments, doing peer review, doing the readings, etc.). But there is a difference between putting content online and teaching online. Anyone can send an email, anyone can put things on a CMS, but teaching online requires more than using a technology tool to facilitate or enhance your teaching. Our experience led us to write this book. We saw that what we were doing in our online courses was architecting an experience for our students and for ourselves and because of this some patterns began to emerge. We began to see what we were doing in our own classes was leading to some very real insights about who we were as academics and teachers and we wanted to help others.

This book originates from our initial desire to help others by creating an online writing instructors' resources website. Our creation of this resources website, The Online Writing Instruction (OWI) Community: www.owicommunity.org, has helped online writing instructors across the country gain access to relevant OWI resources and be part of a larger community of online writing instructors through our Twitter and Facebook social media outlets. This book expands on the website resources with a more in-depth discussion of practical application for online writing classes and provides useful tools for the instructors who teach them. We hope to equip readers of all circumstances a well-researched approach to OWI. We hope that readers will be inspired by our PARS (personal, accessible, responsive, strategic) approach and will join, and encourage others to join our community and contribute their knowledge to others:

Twitter: @theowicommuity

Facebook: facebook.com/groups/owicommunity

Creating The Online Writing Instruction Community Website

Following the 2015 *Conference on College Composition and Communication* (CCCC), an idea turned into a reality. While attending multiple conferences in previous years and serving as expert panelists to the former CCCC Committee for Effective Practices in Online Writing Instruction (OWI), we noticed something about the online writing instructors we interacted with: they were under-supported and said they wanted a central resource where they could go for help with administering, creating and teaching their online writing programs and courses.

Between the two of us, we had years of experience designing, maintaining and teaching online writing courses, and years of experience collaborating with some of the well-known scholars in OWI research. Along with other members of the former CCCC Committee for Effective Practices in OWI, we were continually advertising the work of these scholars and the work that the committee was doing to make OWI a legitimate sub-field in the field of writing studies. Based on our committee work and the needs expressed by the beleaguered writing instructors we met, we both felt that a huge hole existed in that there was no one single place, a "go to" resource that gathered all of this great scholarly work on OWI for instructors, especially for instructors without access to the conferences we were attending. So, in 2015, we created The Online Writing Instruction Community (www.owicommunity.org).

In order to give the website the ethos it deserved, we began working out our own approach to OWI. We wanted to develop a philosophy based on our experiences and we wanted this to be something quickly accessible for new or under supported online writing instructors. We desired to create something that would help encompass all of the approaches to OWI that many successful instructors and administrators take, and so (alongside the creation of The OWIC website/ social media group) the PARS approach to OWI was developed. PARS stands for:

- **Personal**
- **Accessible**

- **Responsive**
- **Strategic**

We feel these four concepts encompass the most important elements of past and current research and theory on OWI. We hope that by providing a specific OWI focused approach, one we call PARS (personal, accessible, responsive, strategic), administrators and instructors will be able to see that they can utilize skill sets they already possess and learn helpful strategies in order to face a potentially new landscape for them, the online writing course. With the PARS philosophy, we draw on some very basic but fundamental best practices of writing instruction. We, like many, hold the following beliefs:

- Instructors of any subject need to be **personal** and personable
- Instructors and content need(s) to be **accessible** to students
- Instructors have a duty to be **responsive** to student queries/requests for help
- Instructors should be creative and **strategic** in their pedagogy and with the design and administration of their writing courses

While these may seem like common knowledge and very simple best practices of instruction, we feel they are core keys to success for online instructors and we see the benefit that these elements (personal, accessible, responsive strategic) could offer administrators of online writing programs as well. We offer this book in the present state of the OWI field as a useful guide for new and seasoned online writing instructors, graduate students, and administrators. We have already seen our community reach many overwhelmed contingent online writing instructors and we have experienced the excitement they have expressed to have a place to go for help. We've witnessed some great conversations about OWI in our social media groups and we've networked with a lot of new scholars at conferences. We hope that this book will be useful and will help you think about the experiences you're creating for your students through the online writing courses you create, instruct, or administer. Up until this point, there has not been a book written with one distinct approach to OWI. We feel that providing a balanced and supported approach that encompasses the theory and practice from decades of previous research will help to develop a new generation of online writing instructors.

Why PARS?: The Merging of Golf and OWI

The PARS philosophy to OWI was created initially out of a shared interest in the game of golf. We both play and watch televised golf a lot. We're not saying we're good (well Casey is!), we just like to watch it on TV and play for fun! We wanted a term that would support our philosophy of OWI because we feel that no one needs to be an expert going into teaching online, but everyone can improve his or her online teaching/administration/course design game with proper support.

We also wanted to create an acronym (because academics love acronyms!) that would encompass our strategy and approach to OWI, but one that would be easily remembered.

In golf, the term "par" stands for the number of strokes a golfer is expected to take on a particular hole; it's the score a scratch golfer with a zero handicap (i.e., a really good player, not like us!) would expect to make. The total sum of pars on a typical 18-hole golf course is 72, though some can be 71 or 70 (these are usually *really* hard courses). Shooting a par score is a goal for many experienced and inexperienced golfers because it means you had a really good day; you did what was expected, but what was expected was a high level of play. Shooting par on a round of 18 holes means you scored really well and that you're shooting for expert level, but many golfers never reach expert level and that's okay.

Golf is a great game for novices to learn. It's low impact (unless you are trying to swing out of your shoes!), easy to walk or ride (golf carts are fun to drive!), and people hopefully enjoy the game for what it is—a game against yourself. And over time, people who play golf get good enough at the game that a PAR on a hole becomes a reality; with practice everyone gets better. The same can be said for online writing instruction, administration, and course design. When we play (teach, administer, or design an OWI course) and get small "wins" we want to keep going and make ourselves better. When we golf, and when we teach writing in an online setting, we aim to be "par for the course" (pun intended), so the acronym seemed like a good fit, albeit a little cheesy.

As experienced writing instructors, we found that sometimes just setting up an online writing course can be difficult. There are a number of things to contend with such as the Course Management System (CMS) or Learning Management System (LMS) one will use, the documentation, delivery, and translation of pedagogy into the online space. However, we've also found that there are a few things that instructors can do to help streamline the semester and make online classes a better knowledge-making space for their students. The PARS approach is flexible enough to apply to the administration of an online writing program, the creation of online courses and the instruction of online courses. The elements of PARS approach center on the user and their experience which we feel is so important in OWI. Additionally, the PARS approach allowed for an easy way to remember a set of effective best practices.

So why one specific approach to OWI? (or why the PARS approach is relevant!)

As noted, the PARS approach to OWI offers one specific approach to online writing courses, instruction and administration. This approach encompasses a lot of moving elements of the online writing classroom and doesn't aim to provide solutions to every single thing one might encounter in an online writing course. But it does provide guidance on how to tackle some of the more challenging aspects of teaching online and it offers an approach specifically focused on the entire experience (the student and faculty experience of OWI). The combined elements of the PARS approach (personal, accessible, responsive, strategic) allow novice online instructors to develop instructional strategies and course design strategies that help them with navigating the unfamiliar or new aspects of teaching online that are perhaps easier to address in F2F teaching:

- Cultivating relationships virtually with students (Personal)
- Creating an identity and presence as an online instructor (Personal)
- Setting boundaries for instruction/grading/virtual availability (Responsive)
- Handling the extra written communication (Accessible/Responsive/ Strategic)
- Responding to student writing in digital environment (Responsive/ Strategic)
- Creating an entire course prior to the class ever meeting (Accessible/ Responsive/Strategic)
- Being strategic in pedagogy and facilitation of a course (Personal/ Strategic)
- Cultivating support from the WPA or department chair (Personal/ Responsive/Strategic)

When the four elements of the PARS approach get combined, our hope is that being an online writing instructor can seem more manageable. Similarly to Cargile Cook's (2007) argument that training future online writing instructors in a digital environment is vital, we feel that providing future online instructors with a concrete approach to OWI is just as important (Immersion in a Digital Pool). Having both been thrown into OWI with very little training, we know the value of having specific tools that one can fall back on when some of the more challenging aspects of online instruction arise. We hope the PARS approach and The OWI Community resources website and social media give you some specific tools and a supportive network to do the work you do and create an amazing online learning experience for your students.

Why Community Focused OWI? (or why community is so important to us!)

With The OWIC website (www.owicommunity.org) and social media outlets (Twitter: @theowicommuity, Facebook: facebook.com/groups/owicommunity) we wanted to reach some specific audiences: people who couldn't attend annual writing conferences; people who didn't have existing professional relationships with the OWI scholars; and administrators with little means to train their instructors in OWI scholarship and pedagogy. We wanted to "make the distance not distant" for online writing instructors across the country (Harris, Weber, Borgman, 2016, p. 17).

We wanted to create a community, but not just any community, an online writing instructors' community of new and old, talented, underrepresented, and amazing OWI scholars who could collaborate and share their experiences. We desired to create a community dedicated to fostering connections, sharing challenges, being supported by other online writing instructors, sharing ideas, learning from more experienced online writing instructors, having discussions about the future of OWI, making personal connections through virtual/face-to-face gatherings, and so much more!

Instructor networks like The OWI Community are not a new thing, many exist across the country and within the field of writing studies. Instructor networks "are generally defined as professional communities of educators unified around common concerns that are pedagogical, disciplinary, or reform-oriented in nature, although, upon occasion, networks may address more than one of these" (Swenson, 2003, p. 277). These instructor networks, or communities, offer many benefits to their members, including opportunities for professional development, opportunities to learn from others' professional experience, networking for employment or graduate school, and sharing ideas and instructional strategies to name a few.

There is a rich history of OWI in the writing studies field that dates back more than thirty years. The surge in online writing instruction has been made possible by a group of folks that saw the potential of taking writing online and experimenting with early adaptations of mixed or hybrid courses. We were both inspired by and influenced by some of these early adopters and have had the pleasure of working with them for many years. Discussions about community in online writing instruction have been happening for thirty plus years as well but community has always been a challenge for instructors teaching online writing courses. In fact, the conversation of creating a supportive community for instructors using computer-based writing instruction began as early as 2000 in Harrington et al.'s *The Online Writing Classroom*, and this call for a supportive community has been discussed as recently as 2015 in Hewett and DePew's *Foundational Practices of Online Writing Instruction (OWI)*. In his book *Teaching Writing Online: How & Why*, Warnock (2009) notes that composition as a field has a long history of idea sharing, "Education, and writing instruction in particular, is dynamic: people are inventing new ways daily to help students learn" and he suggest that the online environment is an ideal space to share resources across departments and the whole discipline because it can "leverage . . . technology while saving costs by the use of what Marsh, McFadden, and Price call reusable learning objects (ROL)" (pp. 163–164).

In noting this long history of writing instructors learning from other writing instructors, Warnock (2009) argued for the need for a digital community space for online writing instructors to "share our resources as teachers so as to maximize the best practices of instruction and to refine our own approaches" (p. 166). These types of community spaces appear present in OWI scholar discussions from 2000 to 2015. The concept of community spaces is noted in a 2000 piece that discusses a 1995 *Computers and Writing* workshop where leaders of the workshop used a MOO (Massive Open Online space) to involve people outside of the conference in their workshop discussion, "Our goal was to compile strategies for survival in the often-wild world of the computer classroom" (Coffield et al., 2000, p.286). Following the conference, the conversation continued, "we have continued that workshop's conversation on national electronic discussion groups, as well as on World Wide Web" (Coffield et al., 2000, p. 286). But online community discussions came even earlier than this with Fred Kemp's alliance for computers and writing founded in 1990, which attracted graduate students, professors and others doing work with computers and composition. This type of network facilitated and sustained a discussion that happened at the conference and further allowed for a continued support network of the individuals present at that conference.

Adding to the potential of community spaces, others have addressed how these spaces can help address sustainability, "Increasing the knowledge flow about teaching practices has the potential to alleviate issues with teaching online as well as improving teaching practices in all courses, thus leading to sustainable pedagogical practices that will enhance programs and curricula" (Meloncon & Arduser, 2013, p. 88). Sustained pedagogical practices allow for seasoned online writing instructors to train new online writing instructors who are often faced with a multitude of challenges related to moving to the online domain. Pedagogy and professional support are challenges that are never ending. These are an ongoing struggle for many departments that need constant reinvention due to new audiences emerging. The growth of OWI instructors exploded in the past fifteen years and the older communities are not enough to support this new OWI instructor audience. Many scholars have discussed various options for these shared instructor spaces (Coffield et al., 2000; Hewett & Ehmann, 2004; Mechenbier, 2015; Meloncon & Arduser, 2013; Warnock, 2009) and some of the options discussed include: instant messaging, synchronous group chats, email and listservs as ideal virtual spaces that help instructors to talk about the work they do on a daily basis.

In crafting The OWI Community and social media space we aimed to fill this gap of lack of community support for online writing instructors, especially those that are contingent and work for multiple institutions. Both of us get annoyed at the pretension of academia so we wanted to create a site that was inclusive for everyone, a site that reiterated that everyone mattered. Tenured, non-tenured, contingent, two-year college, whatever one's status, we wanted people to feel welcome to join our site and our larger conversations about OWI. We wanted to become the go-to place for online writing instructors. We wanted to be the answer to the question: are there any resources for online writing instructors that I can access and maybe connect with the people who created the content? The two of us had a strong desire to offer open access resources and not charge for our services. So many people try to capitalize on their good ideas, but we just wanted to help others like ourselves and reduce the frustration and anxiety of being a new online writing instructor. We've been there. We've both jumped into our first online writing course head first and we knew how challenging it is and how lonely it can feel to be out in cyberland. We tell our students to find resources to help them, and when they can't, then they should try to create them. So, we did that! Our site comes down to the basic idea that we want people to know they are not alone. Our aim is to provide a space for people to share ideas, pedagogies, and tools regarding OWI, and start conversations on where OWI is going. Our colleagues have referred to us and our site as "grassroots" and we take this as a huge compliment. It means that we've met our goal for the site, that we've created a safe inclusive space for all instructors who teach writing online to share ideas, glean new insights about OWI and feel a part of something bigger, to feel like the belong to a community who shares their passion and interest in OWI.

Timing is Important: Resistance and Acceptance of OWI

The turn of the century brought fears of the Y2K virus, an election where one candidate was teased for inventing the Internet, and the beginning of the surge in online higher education courses and degree programs. In the early days, many were hesitant to sing the praises of online courses, especially writing instructors and administrators. Teaching writing has always been personal for faculty and learning to write has always been personal for students. Sometimes the connections that students make with faculty members are pure and honest while other times they are fraught, but there is no denying that the feedback-driven nature of writing instruction brings students and faculty together in a way that makes it more personal than other courses. For many writing instructors the sheer act of teaching is personal because writing instructors learn to teach writing by doing and by failing forward (teaching for the first time and then repeating the process with new knowledge). Most writing instructors start their first class having never had the opportunity to teach much of anything in terms of topics and content. Writing instruction becomes a process of growth where novice instructors are honing their pedagogy alongside the student who is growing their own writing skills. Both instruction and learning to write are a collaborative process, a team effort of give and take (like an alternate shot contest in golf!). Teaching someone else to write is a huge undertaking just as writing well is difficult, and learning to write better is a personal journey and can be a struggle. Because of this, so many instructors value the F2F time to help coach students and encourage them to have more confidence in their ability to write—this can also give the instructor more confidence as well.

For many instructors, the classroom workshop model is not something one can digitize—it is organic and incompatible with anything that might become a barrier to peer-to-peer, student-to-instructor learning. However, while many writing instructors have embraced the technological advancements of computers to facilitate word processing (information dissemination), and thus allowing digital technologies to impact their writing instruction, many are hesitant to see writing instruction go entirely online.

We know from experience that it is difficult to shift F2F instruction to a digital space and we both have our reasons for becoming online writing instructors and supporting the OWI sub-field of writing studies with our own research. But while the acceptance among some faculty of online courses remains skeptical, more faculty are open to teaching online, some even eager to do so (especially contingent faculty). Some faculty have a desire to teach online because they see it as a way to try out new ways of teaching or they feel there are better ways to teach certain concepts digitally versus F2F. Others choose to teach online because they are the only ones in their department with the willingness to try, and others begin teaching online because they desire a more flexible schedule for accessibility reasons. But no matter where faculty stand—from skeptic to enthusiast—researchers agree on one thing: faculty acceptance of online courses is imperative to success and there "is a strong relationship between the reported level of acceptance among faculty members and the number of distance education students at that institution, with faculty at institutions with larger numbers of distance students being more accepting" (Online Report Card, 2015, p. 26). The field of writing studies as a whole is moving towards acceptance, but it has a long way to go in making quality online writing courses a priority.

Both of us started out as hybrid or blended instructors (teaching F2F with so much of our content and student interaction happening online), really, as we used e-Learning components in our early F2F courses. While in graduate school at Western Michigan University, Jessie used a hybrid course structure by combining regular class meetings with online discussion boards in her F2F courses of first-year writing. Moving the discussion outside of class allowed for more enriched discussion during their scheduled meetings. It also forced students to really digest readings they were assigned because they were engaging with them in multiple ways. As a graduate student at Ball State University, Casey centered all of his student feedback and peer review within course blogs so students could review writing online and use class time for discussion. By moving the initial peer review discussion online, it gave him an opportunity to see feedback students were providing each other at an early stage in writing and focus the next lesson plan around what he saw in the responses.

We saw, and still see, such digital technology as an opportunity to take advantage of online spaces already being used by students and refocusing them for improving writing. We saw what Warnock (2009) pointed out in his book, *Teaching Writing Online: How & Why*, "As composition teachers, we may have an inherent advantage, which is another reason that we, among all teachers, should be at the forefront of investigating online teaching possibilities: we are already accustomed to student-centered courses" (p.29). We see this advantage and we hope that you will too.

We've self-taught ourselves one too many times on basic skills and strategies. We've been contingent laborers. And so, we offer this book by no means as a panacea for the many issues so many people believe ails online writing instruction, however, we view this text as an aid for new and under-supported instructors everywhere (like us) who are trying to figure out how to move their writing instruction and writing courses from F2F to the digital environment in a way that helps students. We have both been under-supported instructors at one point in our careers and so we write from our own experience and the struggles we endured. Based on those struggles, we believe that having a specific OWI approach or philosophy and a supportive community can help address the missing support that leaves many new and experienced OWI instructors bereft. As we have attended conferences and worked with influential OWI scholars over the years, we know the value of getting involved with like-minded individuals, but we also know that collaboration is not available to everyone, so thinking back to those days we decided we needed to create a new opportunity to provide this type of community support to individuals who were not able to attend conferences or network with OWI scholars as we have done.

You're not alone! Let's craft an identity together!

The classrooms discussed in the 2000 piece above (about the 1995 *Computers and Writing* workshop, Coffield et al.) were facilitated by instructors using some of the first computer-based instruction models of modern online writing courses. The authors note how these "early adopters" were often forging the "road not taken" and "feeling isolated and alone" (Coffield et al., 2000, p. 285). Feelings of isolation can affect online writing instructors more than F2F ones due to the nature of working remotely or the nature of teaching solely with computers. This feeling of being alone is not far off from a current view of OWI in some departments across the country; as not everyone has bought into online courses. Many educators around the country who teach online feel a sense of isolation in their quest to teach writing online and often many feel like they need to defend their choice to teach online over traditional face-to-face instruction. We've also felt this way from time to time in our own careers as online writing instructors and contingent laborers.

It's a known fact that contingent faculty are often relied upon to teach online writing courses more frequently than full-time or tenured faculty. Contingent faculty are an overused and underappreciated demographic of instructors used heavily for online teaching and unfortunately their status within a department can sometimes prevent them from feeling a part of the department. "They exist on the periphery of the campus community, they often do not know each other personally, and they are competing with each other for courses (and income). Developing a community—even a virtual community—will promote collegiality and a sense of being *part* of the department" (Mechenbier, 2015, p. 238). Add to this job uncertainty and fluctuating enrollment and a contingent faculty member might be less inclined to ask for help or seek support from those who may or may not renew their contract.

In creating our site and social media groups, we found that there has been a long discussion in the field of writing studies that those who do work with computers and writing have felt isolated or outcast in their department; this is an ever-present feeling for online writing instructors and most apparent for contingent faculty as noted above. As people who enjoy computers and were early adopters of some of the first ever learning management systems, we have felt this isolation. Leaning on others who shared our passion for technology helped us grow our knowledge. We wanted to be that type of support for those who have never taught online but were interested in it, or those that who were forced to take the online course because no one else wanted it. We really feel that learning from experienced online writing instructors helps inexperienced instructors learn and grow their ability to teach students in online contexts. This type of mentorship model is used as graduate students learn to teach writing courses in their first year of a program, and while it's not currently used for all new online writing instructors, a community is essential in supporting those that don't have this type of mentorship to learn from experienced online writing instructors. We felt that we could recreate this model with our OWI Community site and social media groups.

As we continued to research, we found that underlying the various calls for community (in OWI or community for those who teach with computers) seemed to be a desire to share knowledge, but also something more—a need to feel validated/legitimized for the work one is doing; a need to be a part of something. These shared spaces can be ideal to share strategies and practices for OWI, as well as sharing content and sharing dialogue about the challenges and successes of online writing courses. Those without a home institution or those stringing together work at multiple institutions especially benefit from instructor to instructor camaraderie, "contingent online faculty also benefit from [a] sense of community and connection with other instructors; teacher satisfaction improves when faculty have a sense of contribution . . ." (Mechenbier, 2015, p. 239). This need for a sense of belonging or working together as a team underlies a lot of the conversations we've had with online instructors at conferences. Online writing instructors want to share information, course content and strategies, and work with others to alleviate some of the burdens faced by new online instructors. We wanted to do this too but even more so we wanted to help people feel like they belonged to a community that reiterates that their work has real value.

A call for community spaces in online writing instruction is present and has been present in the past, but what remains is a real question of do people want it? This helped guide us as we sought to answer this question and we found early on as we advertised our site, that yes, indeed, people want to be a part of a community, even if it is virtual. This desire for a sense of community has created the need for such spaces and has called on educators and administrators to provide them and/or interact within them. There have been countless ways that those community spaces can be realized and/or assembled, and there have been multiple discussions on the benefits that these community spaces offer to faculty of all levels, but specifically contingent faculty. With The OWI Community (www .owicommunity.org) and the PARS approach to OWI, we hope to offer an opportunity where we can learn and grow together.

Structure of the Book

This book was designed with several audiences in mind. We want to provide a practical guidebook that includes a distinct approach to OWI for new and/or existing online writing instructors who are under supported in their current position and don't have a lot of time to devote to learning more about OWI theory and practice. And in doing so, our book can also be used to inform administrators how to add online courses (or sustain the ones they have already added) to their writing program with success. We envision this book being used by instructors of graduate level courses who are teaching students how to teach writing online. We see the potential for this book to be used in classrooms to introduce graduate students to a specific OWI approach and philosophy and even prepare them for becoming Online Writing Program Administrators (OWPAs) (Borgman, 2016). We feel these audiences will benefit the most from a book that focuses on a specific approach to OWI. We feel that offering a book specifically on The PARS approach to OWI can offer a fresh perspective to the sub-field of OWI and really compliment what has already been written on the subject. While a lot of valuable books exist on OWI, the goal of our text is to offer one specific approach to OWI (the PARS approach: personal, accessible, responsive, strategic), which instructors and administrators can easily use and integrate into their online classrooms.

The book format is simple and includes: a foreword (which hopefully you've already read!), this introduction chapter, a chapter for every element of the PARS (personal, accessible, responsive, and strategic) approach, a conclusion chapter, and an afterword (which we hope you will read!). Spoiler alert! You will find that once you finish the book, the PARS approach is based in user experience (UX) and we'll argue throughout that really, the key to OWI is designing a great user experience for instructors and students alike.

We have put in some stories along the way, some examples of our own experience so you can see you are not alone in fumbling your way through online teaching. Each of the PARS approach chapters begins with "On the Tee!" a quick chapter preview to define the PARS letter for that chapter. Each of the PARS chapters provides many brief personal vignettes about our own experience being an online student or an online instructor and in each PARS chapter we attempt to ground the concept in the Theory, Practice, and Significance to OWI, in which we discuss the theory and research behind the concept, why the concept matters to OWI, and illustrate how the concept can be applied to the online writing classroom or inform online writing instructor pedagogy. The remainder of the PARS chapters are divided into three sections: design, instruction, and administration, and in these subsections, we outline how the specific PARS concept works with regard to the design, instruction and administration of online writing course. The PARS chapters also include a bonus "Drive for Show, Putt for Dough" segment in which we discuss bonus activities or strategies we utilize in our own individual online writing courses. We call it that because in golf anyone can hit it really far, but the short game, like putting and chipping, is where you really make your money and save your game in the long run. Hence, drive for show (hit it a mile, it looks nice), putt for dough (this is where the golfers show their skill). Essentially, the more precise and focused you are with your short game, the more successful you will be in the long run.

At the end of each chapter, is a key takeaway, titled "For the hole in one!" in which one specific element of the chapter discussion is reiterated. We call it "For the hole in one!" because that's every golfer's dream (to hit a hole in one shot) especially new inexperienced golfers. This title also puts the focus on one, one key thing. We envisioned our reading audiences in need of quick practical advice, so we sought to provide quick and easy "if you do this one thing" approaches at the end of each chapter to drive home the most important point of the chapter and address this need for practical tools. We included this final key takeaway in order to provide readers with quick solutions to common OWI challenges and to highlight ways to enact each of the PARS concepts in an online writing course.

References

Allen, I. E. & J. Seaman. (Feb. 2016). Report Card: Tracking online education in the united states. *Babson Research Group*. (pp. 1–62). Retrieved from http://online learningsurvey.com/reports/onlinereportcard.pdf.

Allen, I. E. & J. Seaman. (2017). Digital learning compass: Distance education report 2017. Retrieved from https://onlinelearningsurvey.com/reports/digtiallearning compassenrollment2017.pdf.

Borgman, J. (2016). The online writing program administrator (OWPA): Maintaining a brand in the age of MOOCS. In K. Blair & E. Monske (Eds.), *Writing and composing in the age of MOOCS* (pp. 188–201). Hershey, PA: IGI Global.

Cargile Cook, K. (2007). Immersion in a digital pool: Training prospective online instructors in online environments. *Technical Communication Quarterly, 16*(1), 55–82.

CCCC Committee for Best Practices in Online Writing Instruction. (2014). A position statement of principles and example effective practices for online writing instruction (OWI). Retrieved from http://www.ncte.org/cccc/resources/positions/owiprinciples.

Coffield, K., Essid, J., Lasarenko, J., Record, L., Selfe, D., Stilley, H. (2000). Surveying the electronic landscape: A guide to forming a supportive teaching community. In S. Harrington, M. Day, R. Rickly (Eds.). *The online writing classroom* (pp. 285–317). Cresskill, NJ: Hampton Press.

Harris, H. Nier-Weber, D. & Borgman, J. (2016). When the distance is not distant: Using minimalist design to maximize interaction in online writing courses and improve faculty professional development. In D. Ruefman & A. Scheg (Eds.), *Applied pedagogies: Strategies for online writing instruction* (pp. 151–181). Logan, UT: Utah State University Press.

Hewett, B. & Ehmann Powers, C. (2004). *Preparing educators for online writing instruction: Principles and processes.* Urbana: NCTE.

Mechenbier, M. (2015). Contingent faculty and OWI. In B. Hewett & K. DePew (Eds.), *Foundational practices of online writing instruction* (pp. 227–249). Fort Collins, CO: The WAC Clearinghouse and Parlor Press. Retrieved from https://wac.colostate.edu/books/perspectives/owi/.

Meloncon, L. & Arduser, L. (2013). Communities of practice approach: A new model for online course development and sustainability. In K. Cargile Cook & K. Grant-Davie (Eds.), *Online education 2.0: Evolving, adapting and reinventing online technical communication* (pp. 73–90). Amityville, NY: Baywood Publishing Company.

Newbold, W. (2015). Preface. In B. Hewett & K. DePew (Eds.), *Foundational practices of online writing instruction* (pp. xi-xv). Fort Collins, CO: The WAC Clearing-house and Parlor Press. Retrieved from https://wac.colostate.edu/books/perspectives/owi/.

Swenson, J. (2003). Transformative teacher networks, on-line professional development, and the write for your life project. *English Education*, (July), 262–321.

Warnock, S. (2009). *Teaching writing online: How & why.* Urbana, IL: NCTE.

Chapter 1: Personal

On the Tee! The **P** in PARS stands for **Personal**. We feel being personal is one of the most important things you can do as an online writing instructor. Personalizing the classroom, your instruction, or (if you're in administration) the way that you handle your writing instructors is key to success. We encourage you to consider the myriad of ways you can be personal as you develop your OWI practice.

Personal OWI: Theory, Practice, and Significance to OWI

We all have had that one professor who went out their way to connect with us. In fact, these connections might be the very reason we're teachers now. Jessie remembers a time when a professor called her on the phone after some emails they had exchanged regarding Jessie's concerns about the class. Because the instructor thought Jessie was struggling, she wanted to make sure she was okay and was getting the help she needed. Casey remembers his first Ph.D. class where the professor went out her way to work with him and help make connections between his background in creative writing and literature with rhetoric and composition—he understood Hurston and Vonnegut just fine, but Burke made no sense to him (and still doesn't!).

When it comes to creating and teaching an online writing course one of the biggest obstacles, you'll encounter is that you cannot duplicate the face-to-face class. As much as you may want to and as much as you may try, it's just not possible because the experience occurs in a very different medium. However, we do think you can get close to mirroring some of the best elements of a writing class and share in the joy of learning as a group of developing writers. We believe that if you take steps to make online spaces personal and inviting, as you would if the students were physically present, you can drastically change the experience your students have with learning to write in a digital classroom. It's incredibly important to be personal and show your students who you are and that you are there in the online classroom with them; that you're part of the experience with them. As instructors, we like to emphasize that we are here to help! We go out of our way to encourage students to take us up on our offers for help and students like when you are there to help. Strategically emphasizing that you're there to help them goes a long way but in an online course this gesture goes even further because of the isolation many students feel.

Yet, online writing instruction doesn't have to be impersonal or isolating just because you never get to actually meet in person. In fact, being personal is one of the most important things you can do as an online writing instructor in order to forge connections with your students. Warnock (2009) illustrates this by arguing that "Writing instructors have a unique opportunity because writing-centered online courses allow instructors and students to interact beyond content delivery . . . to build a community through electronic means" (p. xix). We want to encourage everyone to capitalize on this "unique opportunity" and make a concentrated effort to create a personal student user experience.

Whether we like it or not, the act of learning to write and the act of writing are fraught with emotion; these are incredibly personal processes. When we teach face-to-face, we can address this emotion with students through our tone of voice, body language, sharing of personal struggles with writing, etc. When writing instruction moves online, connecting with students proves more challenging, so that's where being personal in specific areas of the course can help to create similar connections as one would in a traditional face-to-face course. Sharing your own struggles with the students in the introduction discussion or your professor biography goes a long way in showing students that you acknowledge that writing is an emotional journey. Writing is personal and teaching is personal—connecting with students is a way to confirm students understand various elements of the course. With this comes the need to provide more direction to the students and guide them through the online space. When a student responds to a question in class of "Did that make sense?" with a "Yeah." We can tell if the student is saying "yeah" to confirm understanding or if they are saying "Yeah?" to confirm confusion and it's important to pay attention to these subtle nuances. In online courses we have to decode student responses in email and discussion posts which further complicates our ability to see if they are "getting it" or if they need more help but are afraid to ask.

When you open your courses, you should remind students that when it comes to an online class compared to a face-to-face one, the type of workload can be similar, but the time and energy spent on that workload is likely triple because of the additional text/reading and the lack of normal clarification and interaction a student might get from attending a physical class. You will find that some students may initially believe that an online course is easier to take. Thinking back to our undergraduate days before most classes were being offered online, there were "self-paced" classes (correspondence classes) where the instructor would hand out the schedule, due dates, office hours, and that was it. The concept of "self-paced" was quickly replaced with "fast-paced" as the professor was rarely around and due dates piled up. Unfortunately, online courses (especially poorly designed ones) have kept a little of that correspondence course presence to both students and outsiders. Many still view online courses as correspondence courses and students are sometimes surprised when they enter an online course and they actually have restricted due dates, access and forced interaction with their peers. By creating a personal approach to your class, you can mitigate some of that false correspondence course appeal to the online writing course. You can make it clear that your course is similar to a F2F course and that students will be expected to act and interact as they would in a F2F course. Focusing on creating a personalized course can position you as a guide who helps students achieve the goals of class at a pace that does not leave others behind or allow others to work in isolation of the rest of the class as the earlier correspondence courses did.

Providing students with a personal learning experience takes additional effort. In a traditional F2F course, students have the opportunity of chatting with their instructor before and after class, during office hours, or during scheduled conferences. These options for contact with the instructor are not present in online courses, so it's important to build them into your course through the course design and through your instruction of the course.

Personal Design

The course design is the first place you can start using personal approaches/elements that invite students on a journey of learning together. Designing a class experience is more than just designing documents (syllabus, writing assignments, etc.). As the instructor you must take a user-centered design approach. That is, the student user must be at the forefront and their needs evaluated (Borgman & Dockter, 2018). Personalizing the online classroom/CMS with images, putting your picture on emails, combining your voice with written feedback, and creating videos that walk students through assignments and lesson plans can help you engage in a personable partnership with your students. These small gestures of personalization can also help establish your *ethos* with your students. By doing these few things, you can create a dynamic interaction and collaboration with your students and bridge lack of face-to-face interaction.

Personality plays a key role in how you approach your online writing course (Hewett & Martini, 2018). We know from experience that not all people are cut out to teach online and some need a lot of extra training to make them great on-line instructors. We encourage instructors to evaluate their own personalities and be honest about the type of interactions they value. If one-on-one connections through office hours or writing workshops is something you value, you might consider how you can build those into your own online courses using web confer-encing programs. We encourage instructors to evaluate their own experiences as a student and reflect on what they enjoyed from each of their instructors' personal-ities. In reflecting on your own experiences it's also important to look at what you value, what your personality type is and how it will translate to the online space, ". . . you should consider how your personality influences the way you interact with your students . . . Students need to 'see' you—and each other—in a certain way to have a productive class experience" (Warnock, 2009, pp. 182–183). When we teach online, we both have inviting personalities and we encourage students through multiple means to interact with us. Sometimes we make them interact with us through writing workshop meetings. Our personalities also drive us to make the classroom design more inviting because we don't want students to be put off when they first enter the online space. We want them to understand that we've worked hard to create this personal experience and we want them to see in the design elements how much work we've put in to make them feel welcome. However, we acknowledge that this takes effort. It takes time, planning, and one might argue, extra awareness to be personal in a space where the very nature is impersonal but there are so many opportunities to incorporate personal elements into your online writing course. In addition to inviting connection, community, camaraderie, aesthetics and sensory experience play a strong role in making a course personal so keep that in mind as you design these online class experiences for your students.

The way in which online courses are traditionally designed and facilitated runs counter to our natural instincts to learn through multiple means (aural, tactile, auditory, visual). Therefore instructors/designers must work harder to create learning opportunities that appeal to the various senses. We know that the importance of learning in "robust, sensory rich environments and engaging activities that bring students into contact with one another is how true learning occurs . . . passive learning is simply not compatible with the way the human mind processes information" (Ruefman, 2016, p. 8). In other words, students are more engaged in courses that have a social sense of community, that include sensory details and engaging material and that pay attention to the entire ex-perience, not just the content to be learned. Addressing the geographical dis-tance in online courses is the eternal struggle and designing an online student user experience is something that takes a little practice. In looking at how global education has evolved, personalizing the classroom can also go a long way in assisting learners of other cultures. In the article, "Cultural Dimensions of Learning: Addressing the Challenges of Multicultural Instruction," authors Parrish and Linder-VanBerschot (2010) adapt Hofstede, Hofstede & Minkov's (2010) cultural dimensions to education, forming the cultural dimensions of learning framework (CDLF). In this piece, they argue for instructors to pay attention to cultural dimensions when designing courses. They note that, "The growing multicultural nature of education and training environments makes it critical that instructors and instructional designers, especially working in online learning environments, develop skills to deliver culturally sensitive and culturally adaptive instruction" (p. 1). Essentially, when designing your online course, if you are personal in your approach to teaching, you will invite these global learners to step out of their cultural-training and become engaged with the course.

Aesthetics play a large part in the personalization of the online classroom. Including an instructor contact card or instructor bio with a picture allows your students to place a face with a name. You can also include an introduction welcome video which allows students to see you as you welcome them to the course. Introductory videos can also be used to help teach students how to navigate the course. Even if your school has a standard course template where all of the course information appears in the same place across disciplines it can help to provide students with an introductory tour in case they've never taken an online course before at your school, or they simply need a refresher on where course elements are located. Using stock images throughout the course is another way to make the course more personal and inviting. Where you place the weekly "to do" list you can place an image of a checklist or an image of a calendar. The office or questions area of the course can have a picture of an office door, or a desk as well as a picture of you (see the Drive for Show, Putt for Dough! example in this chapter). Other options for enhancing the aesthetics of the online course in an effort to create a more personal experience include:

- Providing Direction (instructions, plus audio/video overview)
- Reinforcing Content (making content accessible in multiple formats)
- Offering Constructive Feedback (screen capture, audio feedback) (Ruefman, 2016, p. 12–14).

There are so many ways to make your online course more personal for the students. Spending a little time with the course design and incorporating some of these personal elements will go a long way in helping your students feel more connected to you and to the course material. While these things may seem trivial and minor, they make a big impact on the student user experience. Digital technologies are helping to break the boundaries of geographic difference of online courses but you don't have to be a technology wiz to incorporate some of these small personal elements. Check out The OWI Community (www.owicommunity.org) for quick tips, suggested technologies and other ways to design a personal course.

Personal Instruction

One major criticism of distance education is the lack of personal connection with students. And because writing is such a personal act, online writing instruction proves even more challenging when it comes to creating a personal connection. Every instructor usually develops his or her own way of showing their personality online, but there are several direct ways instructors can make themselves more personable to their students. We have found from experience that because the online course is so disconnected from physical cues (body language, eye contact, voice tone, etc.) students feel insecure and struggle to develop a relationship with the instructor unless the instructor is personal and invites that relationship. We know that in an online course personal connections are harder to come by and those relationships take more effort but we also echo the sentiment that "Interpersonal communication always matters in an educational setting, but it seems so much more crucial in an online environment where most of the talk is conducted textually" (Hewett, 2015, p. 226). Instructing students from a distance requires more work on the instructor's part. It challenges instructors to be their best self in every mode of communication and that's hard! Creating your own strategy for personalized online instruction aids in making the student user experience better and it helps to forge a stronger community bond in the course.

Another way that personalized instruction helps is that it addresses some of the cultural differences and views of power present in global learners. In looking at the power distance dimension in education, Hofstede et al. (2010) note that in some cultures, large-power-distance cultures, the parent-child inequality is continued in schooling with the teacher-student relationship (p. 69). In large power-distance cultures, the authority that parents hold over children is reinforced through schooling and respect is given to the teacher figure, just as it is given to a parent figure. Further, the education that a student receives is teacher-centered (the teacher is the keeper of the knowledge). In small-power-distance cultures, the roles are different and the teacher and student are viewed as equals; the teacher takes on more of the coach role, than the authoritarian role (Hofstede et al., 2010, p.69). In small-power-distance cultures, education is student-centered, therefore students are encouraged to ask questions, argue with the teacher and find their own educational strategy (Hofstede et al., 2010, p.70). We all have had the student say they would rather learn from the teacher since that is "what they are paying for," but by making your instruction personal and engaging, students can move into a more dynamic and collaborative learning space. The personal instruction in the course invites students to engage in a more developed learning community and help to reduce the teacher student power dynamics.

As advances in technology allow connection to happen more frequently, our culture is changing to a global culture and, "As technology continues to evolve, we are no longer limited to physical interactions; we connect with others worldwide, our world becomes smaller, and the boundaries between the real and the virtual dissolve. In this new era of rapid technological advances, the value of creating a sense of presence cannot be ignored" (Lehman & Conceicao, 2010, p. 111). We feel that there are many ways you can show your presence and increase the personal aspects of your instruction. For example, using students' names goes a long way in making your interaction with students more personal. One way to ensure a personal connection with students occurs is to focus on making connections with students during the first week. Warnock (2009) suggests ice breaker activities during the first week of class as a way to help shape one's teaching identity. He notes how he spends a lot of time in the first week responding individually to each student's ice breaker activity in an effort to build a connection with each student surrounding common interests (2009, p. 8). He further argues that "In an online class, brief conversational links with students go a long way toward making them feel welcome and connected. When you teach writing, these feelings can build the mutual respect necessary to work with students on their core writing and thinking skills" (2009, p. 123). In other words, be human!

We feel that one area of the online classroom that is a very easy place to be personal is in the instructor information section, sometimes known as the virtual office. Both of us utilize this space to show to our students that we indeed have a face and we are a human, not a computer. In some online courses the instructor information section and virtual office (area to ask questions) are separated. We prefer a mixed approach that mimics a traditional F2F setting—a virtual office where students can learn about their instructor, connect with him/her, and ask questions about the course. Utilizing a specific space in the course where students can be reminded that their instructor is a human, can find information on how to connect with the instructor and can seek out help, reduces the feeling of isolation that often accompanies online courses. Further, because this space is public for the entire class to see, it encourages other students to join in and ask questions and seek out a connection with the instructor. Personal touches could include: the instructor's hobbies/interests, a photograph of the instructor or his/her family, a warm/inviting tone of the writing, the invitation for students to seek out help and help each other, contact information, days off, etc.

Figure 1.1 illustrates one way to make the instructor introduction more inviting and personal. Including some of your hobbies, interests and a little information about your family helps your students know that you're indeed a real person with real interests and that you have a life just as they do. When an instructor starts sharing his or her experience with writing, such as in a biography introduction to the class it invites students to share their own experiences forming bonds among instructor and student and student to student. Figure 1.1 also illustrates how instructors can create a sense of their presence early on in the course.

I love my job and I love learning about and teaching college writing. I entered the field and became an instructor because writing was always difficult for me. I struggled in both high school and college with writing and with getting my thoughts into coherent texts. I tend to write like I talk, which is all over the place!

As my career has grown, I have had great opportunities to teach multiple sections of college writing both face-to-face and online at several different universities.

I am pursing a PhD in Technical Communication and Rhetoric. So, I'm in a similar boat as you...I'm also in school. I understand that going back to school takes a lot of dedication, time and effort!

In my free time, (if I ever have any), I like to spend time with my husband and my dogs, (all three Scottish Terriers) Gus and Zoey and Luna. I also enjoy watching NFL football, college basketball, cooking great food, trying new recipes, being outside and working out.

I'm looking forward to working with all of you this term!
Please don't hesitate to contact me for help :)

Figure 1.1 Instructor Bio. This figure illustrates a Personal way to create an instructor bio for your online writing course.

Presence in an online course is "social, psychological and emotional" and the reason creating a personal presence is so imperative is that as humans, we are social beings, "When the social aspect is absent, we tend to crave it and look for ways to accommodate its absence. Our social nature is integral in our perceptual process when interacting with others not only in the real world but also in the online environment" (Lehman & Conceicao, 2010, pp. 6–7). Creating this social aspect in your course is possible, but it takes direct effort. One way you could help students feel comfortable interacting is to give them a space (like a discussion thread) where they can post and talk to their peers, share their creative work, pictures, etc. Seeing each other and you (as the instructor) as human beings with real lives helps to support the social bond in online courses. Creating student-to-student and instructor-to student connections early helps to establish a sense of community in the class, striving to create "links" between the students and the instructor helps to "create an audience for students," and in doing so helps bridge the gap of writing to an undefined audience that is so challenging for traditional face-to-face students, and further exacerbated for online students (Warnock, 2009, p.8). As the instructor you can model this social bond by facilitating a discussion based on non-class related topics and help to create "links" and a real picture of a defined reading audience for your students. Casey shows his students who their audience is by creating an instructor information card in the syllabus. By including your contact information and availability, you invite students to communicate with you and reiterate that you are in fact a person, not a computer (see Figure 1.2).

We have seen a lot of insights and strategies for personalizing the online classroom and an instructor's approach to teaching the course in distance education scholarship. Research shows that creating a personal element in online courses can increase retention. In their study on community college online courses and social presence, Liu, Gomez & Yen (2009) found that a constant marker of persistence in online courses was "developing integrated social and learning communities" (p. 172). We have found this to be true in our own work as online instructors. We both have reached out to students to keep them from dropping off in progressing through the course. We have been able to solve many student concerns and issues through a quick phone conversation or web conference. We have seen firsthand the value of these personal interactions instructors can make and we want to reiterate their importance in creating and sustaining a successful student learning experience.

WRA 101
Writing as Inquiry

Casey McArdle
email@email
Zoom address: link to Zoom
Online office hours: days & times

My name is Casey McArdle and I will be your guide this semester as we traverse the rewarding waves of writing, reading, and researching.

Figure 1.2 Instructor Contact Information. This figure illustrates a Personal way to create an online instructor contact card.

This need to feel a connection to other learners proves to be even more important in a writing course as the online course setting forces writing (a very personal thing) to become a very social act. The very nature of online courses makes writing both personal and social because the course is so text dependent. We have found in our experience that students want a social experience, even if it's in an online course; humans are social and they want their courses online to feel social and it's not so much that a class is actually social but more that it gives off the appearance of being a social community, "A student with a positive perception of social presence maintains a high degree of interaction and collaboration with peers, and is more likely to successfully complete a community college online course with a better grade" (Liu et al., p. 173). Instructors should take the lead in making the online classroom a safe space to share their writing by sharing some of their own writing and inviting conversation. Online courses then become a space for sharing very personal stuff and that can be intimidating to students who are already self-conscious about how well they think they write. We feel that instructors can help facilitate safe classroom connections by inviting students to share and interact and see themselves and the others in the course as more than just computers interacting in a digital space. Other suggestions include:

- Demonstrate When and How to Communicate
- Consider Tone in Both Asynchronous and Synchronous Settings
- Teach Through Modeling
- Be a Thoughtful Communicator (Hewett, 2015, pp. 228–249)

Other ways that instructors can facilitate a more personal experience is by emailing students or giving them a phone call when they miss an assignment or just stop participating. We've both had really good experiences helping students get back on track. Students appreciate the extra effort of you taking just a few minutes to reach out and see if they are okay and if there's anything you can do to help them get back on track. We have found small personal gestures such emailing or calling students who just stop participating can also help with retention. They realize that they're not out there alone taking your course in isolation so they become more motivated to participate again. Additionally, we've also found that once you make that contact with the missing or inactive student it encourages more communication. Both of us have had a quick phone call with a student and that broke the ice for the rest of the semester and the student started asking questions and getting clarification on confusing aspects of the course or assignments. As you continue to develop your skills as an online instructor, you will find your own unique ways of personalizing your instruction. The possibilities really are endless.

Personal Administration

Within Personal Administration we feel there are two levels: serving faculty, and in doing so, serving students. While we discuss administration in other chapters, for this personal section we believe it begins with being selfless and treating your faculty and others with respect. This may sound like something that does not need to be said, but in our experience it does. As an administrator you're operating on multiple levels. You're serving your department, your faculty and the students who take your writing courses, you're also a researcher and scholar in the field and likely you have a family and personal interests (Hesse, 2016). All of these things pull at your time and energy but one of the first things you learn as you move into administration is that "it's not about you anymore." Many of your colleagues are not meeting with you virtually to see how you are doing, they have questions and situations they need to share with you and now it's your job to listen. Personal administration begins by acknowledging that your faculty needs you. They need you for training and ongoing support to successfully teach writing courses online, they need you to support them and their students, and they need you to be there for them when teaching feels overwhelming and unfulfilling.

At Michigan State University (where Casey is) there are around 7,000 students in our classes for the academic school year and around 60 faculty (both fixed term and tenure). Casey directs two programs on his own, Experience Architecture and Professional and Public Writing, which have over 300 students and 30 faculty combined (one of the degrees is interdisciplinary, which means he works with faculty from other departments across campus). What these numbers mean is: *please have a little compassion for the admins who are doing everything they can.* Now, that doesn't mean you can't take the initiative to learn on your own and report back to your admin teams what you learned. A colleague of Casey's, Mike Ristich, was tasked by his department to look into what might happen if MSU started to shift around 20 sections of FYW to hybrid. Mike got all of the instructors for the hybrid classes together, created a hybrid support group, gathered all of the research he could find, came up with some strategies, did a few surveys, and now meets with faculty and deans across campus to share his results. He then created support documents, protocols, and other resources for onboarding new hybrid faculty and administrators. The research he is conducting could help shape the way the university offers hybrid and online courses in the future.

Personal administration begins with treating your faculty with respect and acknowledging that they are contributors to the larger field of writing studies even if they are just instructors and not producing scholarship or presenting at conferences. Teaching is a contribution to the field and it's your job as the administrator to support and acknowledge their contributions. Building personal relationships with your staff is a way to create a better experience for all.

> As a WPA, you don't just impact the way writing is taught as part of the general education curriculum; rather, you shape the campus-wide writing culture, especially with the help of others. Taking the time to build these relationships helps open avenues of future collaboration on writing related projects. Taking the time to build these relationships makes everything you do on campus easier. (Graziano, 2016, para. 4)

Building personal relationships helps facilitate coaching and positions you in a place of both authority (you have much knowledge) and of inspiration (you're there to help make everyone better).

Administering online writing courses and the faculty that teach them requires that you are aware of your audiences (the students, faculty, other school administrators, accrediting bodies, etc.) and respect this diverse group of individuals and their roles in the success of your program. You're creating a user experience for your instructors and your students so it's important to not only be aware of their needs but also respect their limitations. Personal administration recognizes that the skills/knowledge you used to create your own courses can help your instructors create great personal learning spaces for your students. Sharing your knowledge and struggles is one way of being a personal administrator. Respecting your instructors is a large part of directing a writing program but we feel this gets muddied sometimes when administrators are simply looking for someone to take the class (a teacher to fill a slot of the schedule). You will get some instructors who don't care. Okay. So, work with them. Help them find resources that might be of interest to them but still meet the learning outcomes of the program. Depending on where you work, you might have graduate students teaching in your program while finishing up coursework. Help support them. It might be their first-time teaching. Think about that for a minute. It could be their first time teaching *ever* and their first experience is teaching online where the work and stress is double than a traditional face-to-face classroom. Setup bi-weekly video or F2F conferences with your grad students who are teaching in the program—all at once if possible. Make them super informal. Just maybe 10–20 minutes, tops. Check in on them. Make sure they are doing okay. See what you can do to help them with attendance and technology—share stories from when you were in school and had to teach. Help them connect with each other as their cohort goes through the program. Be sure to do all of this for your new instructors as well—especially the ones you just hired. Even if they have taught online before, get bi-weekly video or F2F conference meetings on the calendar, all in a big digital room, and have them go around and share stories. Bring them in. Don't let them sit out there teaching remotely feeling alone. We talk about how important it is to create a community for students when they take our classes online, do the same for your faculty so they don't feel alone.

Being aware of what your department's and your school's diverse audience needs are allows you to be a more successful administrator. Listening to and supporting faculty (so they can support your students) makes you not only a better teacher, but a more personal administrator. Conveying your school's needs also helps you to be a better administrator. Communication with your faculty is imperative and sharing the student demographics, the school's new online learning initiatives, the available resources for online students really helps support your faculty and allows them to be more successful in their jobs because they get a better picture of the school's goals and a clearer picture of the student learner's needs. One way you can share this information is to model for your instructors how to create personalized spaces for their students. You can do this by creating an online course and a video which explains where personalized elements can occur and how instructors can be more personal with their responses to students. Sharing examples of how instructors can be personal using the online teaching training course (if your institution/department has one) is a great place to illustrate the value of being personal to your staff.

As you begin to do this, know that you need training and support as well, especially if you've never taught online before (Borgman, 2016). A WPA that oversees online courses should have the same opportunities for professional development and formative and summative assessment as their F2F teaching counterparts (Minter, 2015, p. 220). Some online writing program administrators have previous OWI experience (even limited experience counts) and if you're one of these administrators you can relate to the struggles online teaching presents. We see value in sharing your struggles with your new and existing online faculty and we feel that doing so opens up a personal dialogue about the challenge that is online instruction. Not everyone gets the luxury of having a person who is an administrator solely responsible for the online writing courses position in their department, an Online Writing Program Administrator or an OWPA, but having someone who can provide guidance and insight on online courses is essential (Borgman, 2016). One inexpensive way to accomplish this is by job shadowing. If you come into your position with no online teaching experience it's important that you get training and that you get some experience teaching online ideally before you ask inexperienced instructors to move into the online domain. If you are lacking in experience, take the time to shadow an online course and understand everything that goes into it. One way to improve your ability to lead others is to get experience yourself and "Having a person with OWI experience in an administrative role allows for an advocate for support for the online writing instructors, especially contingent faculty who tend to be marginalized [and] would help professional development of the faculty who are required to, or voluntarily offer to teach the OWI courses" (Borgman, 2016, p. 199). Being able to be an administrator who can lead by example will improve your ethos with your staff and it will help you to create a better writing program, one that includes thoughtfully planned and facilitated F2F and online writing courses. Shadowing a faculty member helps "improve communication across departments" and it allows you to "gain insight into roles and responsibilities" of others (Manchester Metropolitan University, n.d.). One of the first courses Casey taught involved distance education and by shadowing an instructor for an entire semester before his course began, he got to see how assignments were posted online, discussions, homework, and how the teacher created an engaging learning space, helped him to better understand his online teaching for the next semester and for his F2F courses going forward. This also works for graduate students. If you plan ahead, you have the time to develop faculty and graduate students so they can model the right way to approach OWI and hopefully pass it on as they move into other university spaces. The Online Writing Instruction Community Facebook group (http://facebook.com/groups/owicommunity) is a great way to network and connect with other online writing instructors to shadow or invite as guest speakers to a graduate seminar or lunch and learn for your faculty (if you're an administrator).

Final Thoughts

Current technologies cannot accurately duplicate a F2F environment, which is okay, because we're not advocating that you do that. What we are advocating that you do is create a personal space to engage with your students so that they can get the best learning experience. We have talked a bit about why students take online courses (scheduling, inability to make it to campus, accessibility, social anxieties, etc.) and ideally, they have chosen your online class to learn. By making the experience personal, you are one step closer to helping them reach their goal of learning but you're also allowing them to learn in an inviting environment that allows and encourages them to show their human side. Being personal does so much more than invite your students to be active participants in the course. Using personal elements in your class is the first step in creating a student-to-student and student-to-instructor bond which will facilitate community building in your class for the entire semester. Personalization of the classroom doesn't have to be a huge endeavor, small steps go a long way.

For the Hole in One!

Do an icebreaker activity! In our years of teaching, we've found the icebreaker activity to be the best way to build connections in the first week of the class. If there is one thing to take away from this chapter, it is that making personal connections with students early is imperative. Oftentimes, students will enter an online course with a misunderstanding of what an online course is and that the course will be work at your own pace (correspondence like). Doing an icebreaker activity early in the course allows students to interact with each other right off and helps them to understand the level of participation and response that will be expected. It further helps students to make connections with each other. For example, if your school offers online and face-to-face courses, some students in the online course could be attending campus courses as well and could form study groups for your online course (we've both had this happen!). The thing with icebreaker activities is that they don't have to be elaborate. They can be as simple as "Tell us who you are, where you're from, and why you're in school now" or they can be a game, such as "Two Truths and a Lie," in which students list two things that are true and one thing that isn't and the rest of the class has to guess the lie.

The icebreaker activity also allows you as the instructor to get to know your students because you can find out what they are motivated by, what they might struggle with (time management, confidence in their writing, etc.), why they returned to school and anything else they might want to share with you and their classmates. Further, it allows you to have a casual, but initial sample of their writing; it can function as a writing diagnostic. Icebreaker activities also provide a great opportunity for instructors to be personal. If you create an icebreaker with the goal of sharing personal information, you as the instructor then end up sharing personal information as you respond to everyone in your class and share your own experiences with their topics. For example, when responding to students, we will usually note how we both worked and attended school at the same time and how we understand what a challenge it is to balance so much at one time; this shows we're understanding of the expectations of supporting ourselves and bettering ourselves through learning. Using an icebreaker activity results in a lot of great sharing and commiserating that reinforces the old adage "we're all in this together."

For more practice and application examples, please visit our site: www.owicommunity.org.

Drive for Show, Putt for Dough!

Personalizing the Virtual Office Space

(Jessie)

As noted in our discussion in this chapter, the virtual office is a great space to make personal. In your virtual office, you can invite students to ask questions in order to reduce the intimidation factor, and help them feel like you're there to get them through the course. The office space also helps to reduce duplicate questions (from students emailing) because it directs all questions on the course and course materials to a central location. This central location then serves as another space to build and reinforce the learning community you have set up in your virtual classroom.

In my online courses, I use a picture of my dogs because they are cute (yes, I'm biased!) and I feel like this lets the students into a glimpse of my life outside of being their instructor; a lot of students have pets of their own, so it helps them to create a "link" with me and my love for animals (Warnock, 2009, p. 8). I use this picture where they are both tilting their heads in opposite directions and they look curious. I tag line it with "Did you say you had questions?" I feel like the use of this image is less intimidating than an image of someone writing or an image of a textbook; using one of my own images reduces the stuffiness of the space and makes it inviting.

Additionally, I also like to welcome students to my office space and encourage them to participate in answering questions if they know the answer. I always include my scheduled office hours, as well as an opportunity to schedule another time to meet (by appointment). I include my phone and email address and a reminder that the space is public so anything they don't want the whole class to see should be emailed.

Making it Personal—Hi, I'm a Human!

(Casey)

I have shown you what students see when they log into our Course Management System (CMS) (Figure 1.2), but I also send out a number of emails and links to videos that introduce myself, the course, the week, and the first assignment. For example, my standard email to my students for every online class I teach resembles something like this:

————

Scholars,

Welcome to **Writing as Inquiry**! My name is Professor Casey McArdle and I will be your guide this summer as we explore the ways writing impacts our interactions with our academic, social, and professional spaces.

Everything you need for the class will be hosted in D2L in terms of documents, readings, the schedule, assignments, and videos. We will also be using Eli Review, which you can log into via D2L. This class runs on US EDT time, so make sure that you adjust your schedule accordingly and turn assignments in on time. We only have 6 ½ weeks together so make sure you check the schedule as we will have an assignment due just about every day.

Here is a video that introduces the class: **Link 1**

Here is a video that introduces Week 1: **Link 2**

Here is a video that introduces Project #1: **Link 3**

We will have many videos over the course of the next few weeks and they will be tailored to our needs as we move through the course. If at any time you have a question or would like to talk, feel free to email me or set up a video conference.

Professor McArdle

————

Each video is under four minutes long to keep their attention, which can help to personalize the discussion of the topics and assignments. These videos are by no means the same as interacting with them on the first day of a face-to-face class, but I am reinforcing the fact that I am here, that I am a human, and that I care.

You can use a variety of software, but my OS has built in video screen capture, so I do my videos with a box in the lower right corner where students can see me talking while I walk them through the assignments, the week, the readings, and so on. I do everything I can to have it resemble a video conference and structure it so that I can answer as many questions as I can before they contact me. I also make sure that these videos are closed captioned so they are accessible to students with disabilities and for my ESL students (here they get the video where they hear me speak and can follow the script at the bottom of the screen).

Making these spaces personal allows students to feel comfortable and supported in an otherwise cold online environment. If students feel such personal support, their level of engagement and inquiry will increase along with their success in the class.

References

Borgman, J. (2016). The online writing program administrator (OWPA): Maintaining a brand in the age of MOOCS. In K. Blair & E. Monske (Eds.), *Writing and composing in the age of MOOCS* (pp. 188–201). Hershey, PA: IGI Global.

Borgman, J. & Dockter, J. (2018). Considerations of Access and Design in the Online Writing Classroom. *Computers & Composition, 49, 94–105.*

Hesse, D. (2017). *What is a personal life? In R. Malenczyk* (Ed.), A rhetoric for writing program administrators (pp.473–480). Anderson, SC: Parlor Press.

Hewett, B. (2015). *Reading to learn and writing to teach: Literacy strategies for online writing instruction.* Boston: Bedford St. Martin's.

Hewett, B. & Martini, R. H. (2018). Educating online writing instructors using the Jungian personality types. *Computers and Composition, 47, 34–58.*

Hofstede, G., Hofstede, G. J. & Minkov, M. (2010). *Cultures and Organizations.* New York: McGraw-Hill Education.

Graziano, L. (2016) *Six tips for a successful first year as a writing program administrator.* Retrieved from https://www.chronicle.com/blogs/profhacker/six-tips-for-a-successful-first-year-as-a-writing-program-administrator/62193.

Lehman, R. & Conceicao, S. (2010). *Creating a sense of presence in online teaching: How to "be there" for distance learners.* San Francisco: Jossey-Bass.

Liu, S., Gomez, J. & Yen, C. (2009). Community college online course retention and final grade: Predictability of social presence. *Journal of Interactive Online Learning, 8*(2), 165–182.

Manchester Metropolitan University (n.d.). Job shadowing guidelines. Retrieved from https://www2.mmu.ac.uk/media/mmuacuk/content/documents/human-resources/a-z/guidance-procedures-and-handbooks/Job_Shadowing_Guidelines.pdf.

Minter, D. (2015). Administrative decisions for OWI. In B. Hewett & K. DePew (Eds.), *Foundational practices of online writing instruction* (pp. 211–225). Fort Collins, CO: The WAC Clearinghouse and Parlor Press. Retrieved from https://wac.colostate.edu/books/perspectives/owi/.

Parish, P. & Linder-VanBerschot, J. (2010). Cultural dimensions of learning: Addressing the challenges of multicultural instruction. *International Review of Research in Open and Distance Learning, 11*(2), 1–19.

Ruefman, D. (2016). Return to your source: Aesthetic experience in online writing instruction. In D. Ruefman & A. Scheg (Eds.), *Applied pedagogies: Strategies for online writing instruction* (pp. 151–181). Logan, UT: Utah State University Press.

Warnock, S. (2009). *Teaching writing online: How & why.* Urbana, IL: NCTE.

Chapter 2: Accessible

On the Tee! The **A** in PARS stands for **Accessible**. We view *accessible* similar to its many definitions: "able to be used or obtained," "suitable or ready for use," "available," "obtainable." (Lexico Online). This chapter focuses on how to make your online courses and the content within them accessible for your students.

Accessible OWl: Theory, Practice, and Significance to OWl

Being *somewhat* technically inclined, we've been asked by a number of colleagues to help either upload content online or develop content for them. One example of lack of accessibility that Casey recalls is of a colleague in the early 2000s who was all about putting his course documents online. He made it clear that his face-to-face class would be "almost like it's online!" He was so excited! He used exclamation points in all of his emails! After creating all of his documents, including the syllabus, schedule, assignments, and peer review documents, he uploaded them to the brand new LMS recently purchased by the university. After the first week, he noted that almost all of his students were struggling to access the documents. He asked Casey to take a look, thinking it was the new and expensive LMS. Casey pointed out quite quickly that the issue wasn't the LMS, the issue was that all of the documents he uploaded were saved as Ami Pro files, a word processor that had lost support in the mid-1990s. The instructor was so focused on just putting things online that he never thought about software compatibility, the size of documents for those using dial-up (issues trying to download them), or the sustainable implications of creating an accessible online space for learning. He just assumed that once something was online, then everyone could get it. This example illustrates one of our great observations when it comes to trying to create content to be supported in prefabricated spaces (like a CMS): they have invariably been designed for teachers to use, not students. Casey has even taken time to meet with very large CMS corporations at conferences to talk about accessibility and what it means to design with students in mind. Most of the time he gets promises for change, but as education and time move on, we are seeing that real change happens when instructors are motivated to help students. One thing that you must consider is that as of 2017, the average teacher to student ratio for face-to-face classrooms was 18:1, but as this number increases, it confirms the notion that students are the primary users of the space, not instructors (CampusExplorer.com).

The first of the CCCC OWI Principles states "Online writing instruction should be universally inclusive and accessible" (CCCC Committee for Best Practices, 2014). We appreciate the sentiment in this principle and we know how important it is but as a new online writing instructor or administrator you might be wondering how to make this principle a reality. We believe that if you follow the PARS approach to online teaching and you build your materials from the ground up with accessibility in mind, you will create a learning environment that is more inclusive (Borgman & Dockter, 2016; 2018). But making your course accessible is a huge task and one that requires you to use materials, software, websites, or tools that are not blocked via pay walls, international laws, hardware students might not be able to afford, or any other requirements that eliminate students and their ability to participate at a level necessary for success.

We believe this principle is important given its ethical implications: it is good and right to create an accessible and inclusive space for students. However, many instructors struggle, or avoid, consideration of this principle because they lack the knowledge and experience on how to make things accessible. It takes time to learn about creating accessible materials for students with diverse abilities and it takes time to create an online course that meets the needs of a diverse student population. As Oswal and Meloncon (2017) remind us, "Even when in our teaching approaches we try to integrate disabled students as constituents and stakeholders, our specific pedagogical strategies stop short of being inclusive of the gamut of disabilities represented among our students" (p. 71). In other words, it can be challenging for any instructor to be able to teach completely inclusively to all students they may encounter, but creating awareness and purposefully using accessible strategies are essential places to start.

Creating accessible online spaces can also move you beyond Americans with Disabilities Act (https://www.ada.gov/) (ADA) type accessibility issues because truly accessible online courses means considering schedules, holidays, technical support for students, technical support for you if your computer goes down, or the LMS goes down, and a myriad of other underlying support systems that many universities fail to realize the importance of when offering online courses. What's promising though is that within the last five years or so universities are starting to focus more support systems and put in place these systems that support ADA compliance and student success via web resources and instructional designers. It is in the best interest of universities from both legal and ethical standpoints to be in compliance. We know many of you might not have this support where you teach, and if that is the case, then being proactive can afford you the chance to help your students and help others in your department be more proactive about creating and teaching from accessible content.

We also to want to encourage everyone to expand their definitions of access to include the little things that instructors do that impede students. For example, having too many folders in the CMS, to having too many clicks or links to get to an assignment description, to making the navigation of the CMS too complicated, makes it harder for students to do the work of the course. To us, access isn't only about ADA compliance, it's about making a course that is user-centered and user-driven. A course that pays attention to best practices information architecture and invites students to interact with the course, not be frustrated by endless searching clicking around for what they need to find. It's important to remember that "With the rise of online learning in all forms, academia must continue to change with societal demands and student needs" (Bourelle, 2016, p. 91). We hope that you'll see access like we do as more than just creating accessible content but meeting students where they are and giving them what they need. Many students use their phones for course access, and so many people forget this when they create the content of their online courses. We encourage you to expand your definition of access and think about the ways that you might actually be impeding your students learning by creating barriers to the access of your course content.

Accessible Design

Creating an accessible course begins with an accessible design. Whether you design your own course from scratch or are part of a shared curriculum, there are steps you can take to ensure that the course can be accessed by your students. The design of the course is the first thing that students experience, and if they can't find course content or they are distracted by unnecessary links and clicks, this can impact retention and attention as students may feel it is not worth their time—an internal thought of "Well, if I can't even navigate the course site, how am I even going to manage the course content?"

When we talk about accessible design, one example comes to mind that deals with a colleague of ours who was hired specifically to redesign and implement principles and protocols for a university's current and future online courses. They were like, "Hey, we want you to come here and build everything from the ground up. We know we're not good at this and we really need your help!" When she arrived at the university, she was given complete control over online course design and pedagogy. After six months, she came up with new templates to make documents accessible, she contacted local media labs for video and sound production for the courses, and she secured new webcams and headsets for faculty to have video conferences with students. She had done what she had been hired to do and even more. However, when she completed her research and created the designs and protocols, almost all of the faculty ignored her. They had tenure, she didn't. She was pushing back against a robust machine of faculty who had long lectures via cassette tapes from the 1980s and had converted the poor quality for the web. They also used antiquated and inaccessible documents in the CMS, and in doing so, basically put the course on autopilot while they went on vacation. When she brought all of these problems to their attention, they didn't care. They were getting paid by the class and they had contracts that said they didn't have to change no matter what research she showed them. No matter how much feedback she presented from students in the past who found their courses, content, and pedagogy inaccessible, it was just a job to the instructors. Students were unsatisfied customers filing their complaints to an academic Better Business Bureau that said they cared, when in fact, they did not. Our colleague, fed up with no one doing anything, left to take over program at a larger university and has been quite successful in building their online program. This example illustrates that once again, accessibility is much more than just following ADA guidelines (not that they aren't important!), but with this example we see that being accessible is also about listening to students and helping them.

The technology alone (Internet access, computer ownership, etc.) and the isolated nature of working online creates enough barriers for students, so navigating your course and finding what they need to be successful should not be an additional barrier. Access to technology is great, but with the use of technology comes all sorts of accessibility issues.

The technological basis of online teaching can make the potential to learn an impossibility if the online student cannot locate the course, connect to it, or use and maintain the technology necessary to participate in the class. At the heart of online teaching is the goal of student success, but when students and the instructor are distanced from each other, virtual barriers interfere with teaching and learning, and instruction becomes less personal and potentially impossible (Dockter & Borgman, 2016, p. 215).

Being accessible moves beyond just teaching, answering your emails, and responding to students' work, it is also associated with the course web text and content. Your students are not like you, so matching your pedagogy will be a win for everyone. Moving from face-to-face into the online domain takes a willingness to be flexible and re-evaluate one's approaches, "To survive in this land-scape, [online instructions] instructors must be open to new opportunities and widen their perspectives. To teach in this landscape, they need to take a fresh look at their practice, adapt their course design, modify their teaching strategies" (Lehman & Conceicao, 2011, p. ix). Taking assignments and activities created for F2F courses and just putting them online does not work. Trust us on this one! You must find a way to utilize the environment in which the course resides. If you teach in a computer classroom, you can craft assignments that can utilize the lab, or if you teach in a room with lots of small tables, you can schedule some group work because the environment supports collaboration. But the assignment that works in the computer lab or group table classroom may not be suitable for the online environment. You can have the same learning outcomes, but you need to adapt the assignment to match the space. Online teaching that limits itself to one method, whether that be exclusively alphanumeric writing, audio, or video, will limit the meaning-making potential of that teaching material, with the very real possibility of being inaccessible to students who are not of the abled majority. When an instructor limits communication to that which is written, students who develop meaning differently are left out, further isolated (Dockter & Borgman, 2016, p. 220).

The more inclusive your learning environment is, the more students' voices can enter the space to contribute and learn. Understanding your student users is an essential part about making your course more accessible. Anticipating the needs of your students can help to create a more accessible and universal design. As Oswal and Meloncon note, ". . . each user interacts with multimodality differently depending upon the body they got, the adaptive technology they employ on their end, and the uses they have for multimodality in their repertoire of learning tools" (Oswal & Meloncon, 2017, p. 70). Creating videos, having them closed captioned, providing notes for slides, hosting group video conferences, etc., can help in creating not just a personal learning space, but also an accessible one. Making your course accessible to students can happen by making an effort to help your students feel included in the course design and content. We've both had experiences in web conference sessions where the medium wasn't working for us as learners. Jessie isn't an auditory learner so web conferences for her can't just be a conversation or lecture without visuals. Oftentimes instructors or facilitators don't consider delivery of the content and assume that what works for the F2F environment will also work for the online environment. Lecturing from a notebook for two hours as a form of presentation may work in a traditional classroom or presentation session where the audience is sitting in front of you but in an online setting this type of delivery can create a huge barrier of accessibility of the content. For someone who is not an auditory learner, listening to a professor lecture via notes with no visual cues except the professor talking is very challenging. Creating a space where students can participate in the way that they learn is possible:

> The course environment, in our view, can and should be a dynamic space in which students engage directly in the design and content-creation process. If students see themselves as collaborators in the course design process, they are more likely to remain engaged and to begin to grasp the complexity of the tasks and processes they need to complete in order to learn and grow as writers. (Greer & Harris, 2018, p. 17)

Ensuring that the content of the course is accessible to all students requires planning. Not every student can learn from hearing a lecture, just as not every student would be able to learn from seeing a PowerPoint lecture. However, this delivery of the content comes down to an issue of access and spending time on the front end ensuring that the material is accessible to students in multiple means; it is a common best practice of online courses. Putting students' needs first and finding ways to invite them into the collaborative space that is the online classroom will aid in making the content seem more accessible to the students. Students shouldn't have to ask for accessible content.

Accessible Instruction

Accessible instruction is about more than setting expectations and making you and your course materials accessible to your students, it's also about creating a community of inclusion in your course and inviting students with all levels of ability to interact with you in a way that works for them. As Glazier (2016) notes, making a small change to focus on rapport is a way to make one's teaching more accessible to students. The accessibility of the instructor is one of the key factors in engaging the student in an online course so it's important that they have access to you as their instructor. The amount of time needed to successfully teach and facilitate an online course is greater than teaching a traditional face-to-face course, "It is an irrefutable truth of the online class that it takes longer to teach than a class on campus" (Bender, 2012, p. 154). Demands on time include planning, drafting then finalizing a course shell, ensuring consistency to reduce confusion, creating personal connections with students, emailing, participating in discussions, responding to student writing, and the list goes on. Warnock (2015) reiterates this drain on time by indicating how

> [t]ime is a factor in OWI, and time is necessary to communicate well with students. Initially, the time to teach an OWC can be daunting, as many argue. But I have found that teachers will (or should) develop a vast pool of carefully crafted communications . . . I believe that teachers can leverage their time rapidly in online environments if they use these tools well. (p. 158)

Accessible instruction definitely adds to this time commitment. Accessible instruction lends itself to planning and creating points of contact where you and students are able to connect and engage. Accessible instruction requires planning and adjusting one's pedagogy. Planning for an online course is one way instructors can focus on making the content accessible to your students. However, we promise the time commitment made to accessible instruction will be worth it and will facilitate better/stronger bonds with your students.

A well-planned course goes a long way to support student success. Leveraging your time and working to make yourself more accessible to students while still having a life and not being tied to your computer or phone all the time is a challenge and it requires a continual effort. Contact points should be built into the course. The students should have multiple access points in which they can interact with you as their instructor. In our syllabi we always list our email and our Skype username or Zoom web address. We reiterate that email is the best way to get ahold of us as we check that the most, but we also want to remind students that not all interactions have to be text based and asynchronous. Casey averages about two students per semester that have weekly video conferences. They really don't have any issues with grades or problems with the class, they just want to check in and talk with him. These meetings normally last about five to seven minutes, and unless there are any major issues, and they don't need to be longer than that. Take the time to remind your students, all of them if you can, that you are a human and that you care about their learning. Interacting with students and making an effort to build a rapport with them is not just something that can happen once at the beginning of the course, but instead should happen on a weekly to semi-weekly basis—keep your students in the loop. Rapport facilitates access and making the expectations of the course accessible in multiple means (syllabus language, a video welcome, reiterating discussion expectations along with the prompt, etc.) is a way to help students access the content of the course. Knowing what's expected of them is one thing students want to find out as soon as they login the course for the first time. However, making an effort to build a rapport by providing key information of the course and making it accessible to students also helps with retention because if they see you are invested, they will follow your lead (Glazier, 2016).

The gap between online and in-person retention and achievement can be discouraging. Students face many challenges in pursuing their degrees and, most of the time, instructors cannot do much to help students with those challenges. Creating content that promotes easy access is one instructor-driven method that improves online student retention—one that appears to be especially effective at helping our most at-risk students. Access leads to significant improvements in student success, without additional budget requests, policy revisions, or any committee meetings at all (Glazier, 2016, p. 14). While many use videos and personal anecdotes (which are both great!) to create rapport, instructors should also consider their purpose in using these things to engage students. We both have experienced conversations with colleagues about their online course successes and failures. Jessie has an example where she was talking to someone who was complaining that her students weren't watching the videos she was making for her online courses and when Jessie probed further about the format and style of the video, she found out that this instructor was taping three hour long (yes three hours!) lectures and expecting the students to watch them since they would've had to experience these three hours per class in person had they been in this instructor's F2F course. Now, we're not saying that video lectures aren't a great way to supplement materials in an online course, but again, we want to stress make your instruction accessible to the students. Would you want to sit at your computer and watch a three-hour lecture? What if you couldn't hear? What if the video wasn't captioned? Or captioned well? And even if the video was captioned, you'd have to sit and try to keep up with the captioning for three hours and as we know, sometimes captioning can be done very poorly (Zdenek, 2011). Another factor in the use of such long lecture videos is the challenge of learning styles. What if you have several students who don't learn well by listening (not auditory learners)? Creating three-hour videos and not offering the material in other formats can create an access barrier for these students. **What we're attempting to get at here is think before you do!** There are so many things that instructors do with the best intentions of helping their students but sometimes the best intentions actually create barriers for student learning. Think about your favorite podcast (if you have one) —the great ones have topics and stick to them, and are super focused. The annoying ones say they are going to talk about the history of Rome but then they just mention Latin, and spend the bulk of the time telling inside history jokes to their friends and colleagues who are either present for the recording or the target audience. When you are making your audio and videos, think about your audience and compose them in a way that encourages students to listen and watch it several times because it's great—it's accessible.

Accessible Administration

Support is one of the reasons why we initially created The Online Writing Community website. After presenting at conferences and doing workshops all over the US, the biggest questions always circulated around a lack of support for OWI faculty. At the most recent and largest conference in our field we attended several panels where people kept asking: "Where are there resources for online writing instruction?" When we mentioned our website, several pointed out how accessible the content was and how happy they were they could use the resources. You have to model what you teach! Just as we ask you to be accessible for your students, if you are an OWPA (Online Writing Program Administrator; Borgman, 2016), being accessible for your colleagues is an essential part of administration. There are three main elements of accessible administration: 1) helping faculty resolve problems with students, 2) being there to listen to your faculty, and 3) connecting them with technical support.

The first issues of helping faculty resolve problems with students comes from our experience of how to engage and collaborate with students via digital spaces. It's easy to physically meet with a student if problems arise, but our ability to observe body language and tone is impeded via email and poor video conference quality. Being able to meet F2F with students is something traditional writing instruction takes for granted. The same can be applied to being accessible for your faculty. A part of access and accessibility has to do with getting instructors the tools they need to be successful, and training is an important element of this; "... for the most part, the composition field's approach to teacher training has not evolved to include the pedagogies of online education, particularly that of teaching writing—regardless of genre—online" (Bourelle, 2016, p. 91).

If you do a quick search of how to support writing program faculty, you will come across a majority of the websites that discuss how to handle plagiarism or suggestions for how to craft specific assignments (memoirs, narratives, research papers, and so on). To help developing online instructors get the training they need, Bourelle (2016) suggests that administrators and veteran online instructors take the lead and offer ongoing mentorship as well as pedagogy workshops and technology trainings on the department level. These trainings can cover how to use technologies to enhance one's online course, how to design an effective online writing assignment, how to promote successful peer review (Bourelle, 2016, p. 105). But merely focusing on just assignments and plagiarism alone is not enough. You have to be there to listen and support your faculty through every stage of teaching, just as you would with a student. This is a lot of initial heavy lifting on your part, but as the semesters progress, you are creating more and more advocates for you to engage with new instructors and universities—in the long run, it's actually less work.

The last element of administrative and technical support is one that we argue is an essential bridge for most online writing instructors. Given that the entire class resides online, there will be a number of times where the CMS or email or any other digital interaction will break down. For example, one of Casey's colleagues at Michigan State University didn't get emails for two weeks while the entire university upgraded to a new cloud system. The summer online writing course that she was teaching was only six weeks long—so for a third of the entire course the instructor didn't hear anything from students despite pleas from her (the instructor) via email asking them to contact her with any questions.

Your CMS may breakdown or go into an update, your email may fail, your students may not be able to access content via broken links, they might also not be able to submit assignments if files are too big—have backup plans ready to go for when technology fails you (and it will!). These problems arise every semester and it's helpful to troubleshoot these before they arise so you can help your faculty stay on top of the problems and stay ahead of them. We recommend that you create a list of problems and document the issues through each semester and class and have solutions ready based on successful remedies put in place.

Technical support also relies on your ability to help your faculty create accessible spaces for students. As Oswal and Meloncon (2017) note, "We need to start our WPA work from disability and accessibility. When we do so, we encourage direct participation from our disabled students and faculty in our theory, in our research, in our curricular planning, and in our pedagogical conceptualizations. Starting with access helps to create an ideology of inclusion" (p. 74). This type of accessible administration helps and supports both faculty and students.

In addition to the three areas of accessible administration outlined above we also want to encourage administrators to let go of their own agendas and consider the possibilities that new scholars' perspectives can bring to your program and the courses within in it. We've all been in situations where we felt like our way was the best way because it was the way that it (the process) had always been done. However, as we know this is not always a productive mindset. Encouraging your faculty and staff to bring in their own research and experience as well as passions can go a long way. We agree that administrators need

> . . . to push back against our [their] tacit concepts of effectively modeled course design as equivalent to learning and lay bare [their] philosophical beliefs about experiential online courses to help develop online writing instructors who are open to user-centered design, play, and immersive online teaching experiences. User experience practice and mindset, in short, allow[s] [for a] re-conceptualiz[ion] the learner experience and reshap[ing] [of] the program. (Greer & Harris, 2018, p. 21)

Embrace the idea that being accessible requires you to consider multiple levels of your administrative practices and encourages you to think beyond the content of the program.

Final Thoughts

Accessibility online is more than just creating accessible spaces or making course materials compliant with the Americans with Disabilities Act (https://www.ada.gov/) guidelines, it's also about being present in the course for your students and thinking about their course experience. There is a lot of discussion and focus now on how to create usable spaces for your students and we think many of these discussions on user-centered design, universal design and student-centered learning are tremendously helpful when creating spaces yourself, but if you are at the mercy of pre-constructed systems that the university has paid a lot of money for, we suggest that you do your best to supplement the spaces with accessible content and effort. To guide your quest in creating an accessible online course, we suggest you design and operate from the user experience. Focusing on the student user experience is a key to creating accessible material.

A lot of the issues of access really boil down to your course design and the restraints of the CMS. You don't want the navigation of your course to be a barrier to the students learning. Your course navigation should be simple. The number of clicks a student needs to make should be minimized. The layout of your course should be purposeful and everything in your course should support some underlying goal of learning or facilitating access in some way. We have found through lots of experience of trial and error in our own online courses that the best way to encourage student success in online writing courses is to mitigate confusion. Let's repeat that: *the best way to encourage student success is to mitigate confusion*. Make this statement your motto. User testing is one way to ensure you're minimizing confusion. And we're not talking a full-on usability test here. Simply asking two to three friends, colleagues or even family members, to navigate through your course will help you to identify touchpoints or issue of access that your students might experience and find frustrating or confusing.

Minimize the Course Navigation Choices!

One thing we've noticed as online instructors is that the course navigation can be intimidating or inviting. Minimizing the confusion on the left navigation menu (in the CMS) is one of the easiest ways to help your students feel empowered in an online course. We've found that if students struggle to find things in the online course they get frustrated quickly and they can sometimes give up; they get sick of looking or trying to connect the dots.

Helping your student access the course materials by minimizing the navigation choices and linking to various places or elements in the course will help reduce the frustration for your students. One thing we've learned is that the more opportunities you give students to get lost in your course the more complicated they will make it and the more likely they'll be to give up completely. Clarity tends to mitigate the mind fields or rabbit holes; students don't get lost as much or as often.

Clarity in the course navigation also aids in student success, "Laying out the guiding organizational principles for the course, in addition to delineating clear expectations early on, [helps] students to see how smaller assignments scaffold major assignments and ultimately to stay on track in the course" (Borgman, 2015).

Look at the difference in these two CMS navigation maps:

Home		Home
Announcements		Announcements
Syllabus		Modules
Files		Grades
Modules		Chat
Assignments		Student Services
Quizzes		Ask a Librarian
Discussions		
Grades		
Student Services		
Ask a Librarian		
Chat		

The image on the left is a navigation full of links. This type of navigation would overwhelm students because they wouldn't know where to begin. Keeping your navigation simple like the image on the right is likely much less intimidating to students because there are fewer places to click.

If you are super tech savvy, you can even create a Course Tab that is basically a large Google Document that you can update as needed. This Google Document can contain the schedule and everything linked on that schedule document. Make it so students only have to go to one place to get what they need—give them a learning hub to navigate your class and mitigate confusion. That way, when they ask you where things you, you don't have to go on an adventure yourself to send them various links, you will only have to send them one link!

For the Hole in One!

If you take one thing away from this chapter, we hope that it is when you design a course, you're crafting a unique learning experience for your students and access (in its many forms) needs to be at the forefront of your mind. Therefore, we hope that you'll think before you do and really consider the ways that your content will be delivered and accessed by your students. A common best practice of online learning is to make sure your content reaches students by using all senses/learning styles. Use the tools in your CMS to experiment with a course concept and deliver it in various ways for your students.

It's likely that many of your students will have some experience with the university's Course Management System (CMS). Read up on your CMS and practice whatever activities you can through the student simulator if one is accessible. Keep in mind that you will be doing some tech support whether you like it or not, it just happens. You can even make some short Q&A videos for various scenarios that always arise when you teach the course. Accessing the CMS shouldn't be a barrier to learning. With that said, we highly suggest utilizing what your CMS has to offer and providing content to your students in as many ways as possible so that you reach all learning styles and preferences and it's always a good practice to do a CMS overview video at the beginning of the semester so that your students know where everything is within the course.

Learning Style	Preference for Learning	Online Course Activity
Visual (spatial)	preference for pictures and images that aid in spatial understanding	Image and concept gallery
Aural (auditory-musical)	preference for sound/music	podcast
Verbal (linguistic)	preference for words/speech/writing	Written lecture
Physical (kinesthetic)	preference for movement, hands, sense of touch	scavenger hunt collage
Logical (mathematical)	Preference for logic and reasoning systems	mapping out arguments activity
Social (interpersonal)	preference for learning in groups	teamwork assignment group discussion boards
Solitary (intrapersonal)	preference for self-study/working alone	individual brainstorming activities

For more practice and application examples, please visit our site: www.owicommunity.org.

Drive for Show, Putt for Dough!

Table 2.1 is a sample chart of common problems that we (at Michigan State University) created to help faculty fix various technical issues. We know we are not as good as any university IT team, but these are really handy and helpful for quick fixes. It also helps if you can make your own personal "How To" videos that can walk faculty through specific navigation or technical issues. For example, in an effort to show how to use the MSU Mediaspace that hosts videos and also does closed captioning for all uploaded videos, Casey made a video on how to record a video, upload the video to MSU Mediaspace, and then how to order captions. He sends a link to this video out to his entire department at the beginning of every summer semester and fall semester to remind faculty of this free resource that makes videos and content more accessible for students.

Problem	Fix
I can't get Desire to Learn to let me create a discussion thread for my students.	Link to video
How do I send a report to a student's advisor because I can't get ahold of the student?	Brief step-by-step set of instructions for how to contact advisors and a brief email template for what to say.
The video screen capture software does not work. Any suggestions?	Link to how to use Quicktime video screen capture.
	Link to how to use other software in labs across campus that can do it.
Creating accessible online assignments	Links to how to format Word, Google Docs, PDFs, and PPTs so they are accessible for screen readers.

References

Bender, T. (2012). *Discussion-based online teaching to enhance student learning: Theory, practice and assessment.* Sterling, VA: Stylus Publishing.

Borgman, J. (2015). *Clarity in an online course.* Retrieved from http://cccc.ncte.org/cccc/owi-open-resource/course-clarity.

Borgman, J. & Dockter, J. (2018). Considerations of access and design in the online writing classroom. *Computers and Composition, 49,* 94–105.

Bourelle, T. (2016). Preparing graduate students to teach online: Theoretical and pedagogical practices. *Writing Program Administration, 40*(1), 90–113.

Brady, L. (2001). Fault lines in the terrain of distance education. *Computers and Composition, 18*(4), 347–358.

CCCC Committee for Best Practices in Online Writing Instruction. (2014). A position statement of principles and example effective practices for online writing instruction (OWI). Retrieved from http://www.ncte.org/cccc/resources/positions/owiprinciples.

Conceicao, S. & Lehman, R. (2011). *Managing online instructor workload: Strategies for finding balance and success.* San Francisco: Jossey-Bass.

Dockter, J. & Borgman, J. (2016). Minimizing the distance in online writing courses through student engagement. *Teaching English in the Two-Year College, 44*(2), 213–222.

Glazier, R. (2016). Building rapport to improve retention and success in online classes. *Journal of Political Science Education, 12*(4), 437–456. https://doi.org/10.1080/15512169.2016.1155994.

Greer, M. & Harris, H. (2018). User-centered design as a foundation for effective online writing instruction. *Computers and Composition, 49*, 18–24.

Henshaw, A. (2017). Student-to-faculty ratio: What does it mean? Retrieved from https://www.campusexplorer.com/college-advice-tips/0DC5BEE8/Student-to-Faculty-Ratio-What-Does-it-Mean/.

Oswal, S. & Meloncon, L. (2017). Saying no to the checklist: Shifting from ideology of normalcy to an ideology of inclusion in online writing instruction. *Writing Program Administration, 40*(3), 61–77.

Accessible [Def. 1.1, 1.2, 1.3]. (n.d.). Lexico Online. In *Oxford English Dictionary*. Retrieved January 2, 2018, from https://www.lexico.com/en/definition/accessible.

Warnock, S. (2015). Teaching the OWI course. In B. Hewett & K. DePew (Eds.), *Foundational practices of online writing instruction* (pp. 151–181). Fort Collins, CO: The WAC Clearinghouse and Parlor Press. Retrieved from https://wac.colostate.edu/books/perspectives/owi/.

Zdenek, S. (2011). Which sounds are significant? Towards a rhetoric of closed captioning. *Disability Studies Quarterly, 31*(3). Special issue on Disability and Rhetoric. Retrieved from http://www.dsq-sds.org/article/view/1667/1604.

Chapter 3: Responsive

On the Tee! The **R** in PARS stands for **Responsive.** This chapter addresses how you can develop an approach to be responsive to your students and be responsive to the work they complete for the course. Continually responding to student emails, discussion posts and writing assignments is a lot of work. It takes strategy and time to show your students how much you care about them. Being responsive encompasses so much more than just communicating with students. Being responsive is about setting expectations and following through to show the students you're right there with them.

Responsive OWI: Theory, Practice, and Significance to OWI

We see being responsive as the end game of the previous two elements of personal and available: take time to work with your students. You have made the class personal, established your credibility as an instructor, and made your course accessible. All of these culminate in your ability to respond and collaborate with students. Just making yourself available is not responding or collaborating—responding is responding. You may set the schedule as the means of being available, but you still have to respond. An example of responding can be providing feedback. Returning papers with your comments or writing notes within 48 hours of the submission deadline. This is important for two reasons: 1) students can see instructor feedback on initial drafts quickly, and 2) students are able to see how they did on drafts so they can revise and prepare for the next assignment. While the turn-around time is quick, it is important to capitalize on the ethos an instructor establishes by being there for your students and returning their work quickly.

In an online writing course, there are a lot of written responses occurring as the majority of the course can be text-based. Grappling with the volume of text and the literacy load of an online writing course can prove exhausting, but having a strategy and practice for responding to student work helps to combat burnout and aids in managing the workload. Expectations of both the student and instructor factor into this discussion of being responsive quite a lot. As we discussed the value of setting expectations in the previous chapter, we will continue to discuss setting expectations for responding in this chapter. Instructors need to decide how responsive they will be (the quantity and depth of the feedback they will provide) and what mode/medium (text, digital, audio) they'll use to respond to student work. Instructors should convey how they will interact with student work to the students in their courses.

For example, if you are planning to comment on discussion boards or if you choose not to participate and let the students do the discussing, you should let your students know. If you are planning to provide summative comments instead of in-text comments on a student's paper, this also needs to be conveyed. Students need to know what to expect (in terms of feedback on their work) so that they know how to make the most of instructor comments and guidance. Casey remembers using a discussion board in one of the first CMSs he used teaching online. He posted a question about the reading and asked students to write responses with guided questions: "Pose a question of your own, and go and try to answer a question from two other students who posted in the discussion." Pretty simple. After the first day, Casey logged in and began responding to questions and offering links and supporting resources on the topics. The next day he noticed that one of his students replied to his comment with "Nice try bot!" Casey then recorded an audio file and uploaded it as his response to the "bot" reply with a slight chuckle and noted that he was in fact real, that he was in fact the professor, and that he appreciated the student's "bot" response. When the student posted an apologetic reply, Casey said it was no big deal because most people think he's a bot offline anyway!

Working remotely can be great, right? You can work from home, a coffee shop, outside under a tree, or a library. A few might even be envious when you say, "I teach online," but at times, the reality is that teaching online is a lot more work than teaching face-to-face. In working from home, you have to be disciplined and create structure in the day or risk being consumed by too much work or too little motivation. One of the joys *and* downfalls of teaching online is that the course is always available and students always need a response to some question. Learning and personal growth is happening at all hours; students login and complete assignments on their schedule; instructors respond (at a convenient time for them) to students' assignments, helping them to become better communicators; discussion board assignments that inspire further discussion are ongoing, and so on. Learning is 24/7 and that's exciting and thrilling! But this excitement and continual learning process can lead to burnout in a hurry, especially for the instructor.

Responsiveness, or managing your time and determining when you will be available to respond to students is an important component of being successful as an online instructor, but managing this responsiveness is more than just about posting office hours. Boundaries play a large role in online instruction. Being responsive is about setting boundaries with yourself, your students, and the faculty you support. As Brene Brown (2018) notes, "setting boundaries is making clear what's okay and what's not okay, and why" (p. 39). You cannot be available 24/7 for your students, but you can set aside time each day to address a number of issues and problems that arise. Responding in online courses presents new challenges for instructors, especially those who are used to responding face-to-face, via hand written comments, or having conferences with students to discuss their writing. Often, instructors will fail to adapt their response approaches to the online domain or they overcorrect their approach and respond more intensely than they do in their traditional face-to-face courses:

> Selecting appropriate teaching strategies for managing workload, therefore, is necessary to help instructors best allocate time and find balance in their work and personal life ... Teaching online gives instructors more flexibility in terms of where and when they can work, but it can also be a trap unless they allocate their time strategically . . . Time allocation strategies are a necessity for online instructors. (Lehman & Conceicao, 2011, p. 90)

It's important to convey to your students how they can expect their instructors to respond and guide them as they complete their assignments. But it's not all just about the students and instructors—there are multiple stakeholders involved in online writing courses. It's just as important for administrators and program chairs to be responsive to those they support. These stakeholders also have a responsibility to provide advisors, students and their instructors with an understanding of what online learning means at their institution.

Responsive Design

How often do you check your phone? How often do you, in mid-sentence, take out your device and check for messages while talking to someone? Or check your calendar, your email, your social network? If you use your smartphone as much as we do, you can't help but check your email. You never know when a student might have a question about an assignment. You tell yourself, "Well, if I answer it now, early enough in the assignment, that will save me and the student time down the line." While a quick response mitigates confusion keeping up with responding can also wear you down. Here's an example: every summer Casey and his family try to take a small vacation somewhere—it has to be farther than a three-iron (a golf club) from campus to count as a vacation. One of the first times he was teaching two online sections of 101 compressed into a six-and-a-half-week summer session, he was terrified he would not be able to respond to the forty students. So, he replied to every email immediately! After a while he realized that his responses were short and more or less band-aids for larger problems the class was experiencing as a whole—essentially, one student would email him with a question, but by looking over the work every student was doing, he could tell all of the students really should have asked the question. He then noticed that if he sat down at a strategic time and responded in a way that would help *all* students, it would do more for the class that just the quick ones he was sending to individual students. He started to choose quality over immediacy. As he did this, he began to notice the number of questions from students begin to dwindle over the semester as the larger emails to the class answered future unasked questions. He even went a few days without getting an email, which caused him to panic and email Michigan State University IT to see if his email account was down. It was working, as were the group emails he had sent out to his classes.

The reality is that online instruction is not for everyone, "For some students and teachers, online instruction is difficult and even exasperating" (Warnock, 2009, p. xxv). Just because something exciting is available all of the time, doesn't mean being a part of it all the time is healthy or productive. Online instructors run the risk of being overly responsive. The demands of the online classroom, interaction with students, and the sheer volume of work create new challenges that even seasoned online instructors struggle to navigate. One of the greatest challenges for all online instructors is organizing and adapting to the workload of online instruction. Setting times for work is important because "you are not infinitely expandable, and just because the online class is 24/7 does not mean that you are" (Bender, 2012, p. 154). At the start, an instructor new to online teaching may feel very overwhelmed and working harder may seem like the answer. Many new and seasoned online instructors will jump into online instruction with zealous enthusiasm, being available to meet with students with little notice, answering emails at all hours, being visible in the LMS/CMS daily, but this can be counterproductive and sets unrealistic expectations for students while creating an impossible standard for instructors to uphold in the long run. Have you ever gotten an email from a student that read: "Hey, I emailed you two minutes ago? Why haven't you responded?" We have, and when we first started out teaching online, we may have apologized to that student for our lack of attentiveness. However, such approaches for interactions with students are unsustainable.

We know that at times it's easy to feel overwhelmed and check out; to not engage with your students' writing, which is why Warnock (2009) warns new instructors of the challenges of feeling overwhelmed by the demand of responding to student writing, "If at any point you feel overwhelmed and unable to do their shorter, informal writing assignments, then you need to adjust your expectations of how much you are going to respond" (p. 124). In other words, due to the huge amount of text and textual interactions occurring in online writing courses, it is necessary that you change the way you respond to your students; not everything you've done (in terms of responding to student writing) in your face-to-face classes will work in your online classes. You'll need to re-think the design of your course.

Specifically, looking at how you respond to student writing is a start. Ask yourself: is your method of response effective? Can it be translated/adapted for an online course? Courses that reside entirely online have a shifted hierarchy from that of traditional learning space where the instructor is no longer the lead in the class. In online courses, the instructor often acts as a coach or a supportive guide but this shift needs to be made clear to your students. Warnock (2015) reiterates this stating, "Teachers should re-consider how their messages appear to their students, beginning with the initial design and practices in course documents" and he goes on to provide a summary of an OWI group discussion in which participants (all online instructors) stressed the need to lay the "ground rules" and communicate how the course works, including expectations for both students and instructors (pp. 156–157). Laying these ground rules actually helps students understand the digital classroom space as a community of learning. We understand that shifting students' perspective on this role is a bit challenging but it's important for them to see how learning in digital spaces is different because this type of learning and collaboration is more akin to the types of learning and collaboration they'll do in real life once they move on to or continue their careers. Convey to your students through the design of your course that

> [i]n the emerging world of personal learning connections, the online instructor no longer is the sole possessor of the content knowledge. Providing additional resources, while challenging and questioning the student, is part of the instructor's redefined responsibilities. . . . Teaching online is a dynamic process that involves high levels of energetic interaction and quiet moments of contemplation. (Conrad & Donaldson, 2012, pp. 10–11)

Having enough energy to provide effective feedback comes down to managing your time and resources in order to be responsive to students' needs and assist in their growth as writers. In your positions as an online instructor, you have the opportunity to be an audience for your students; an objective set of eyes that responds to their ability to craft meaningful texts. Warnock (2009) notes that "A Key to maximizing the teaching opportunities presented in an online environment is to establish yourself appropriately as an audience for your students. You might assume numerous roles in a class, and these roles shift, but you need to be aware that the way you frame yourself will influence how your students write throughout the course" (p. 1). While it may seem like establishing yourself as an audience for your students seems like an instruction issue, it's actually a design issue. An unclear audience is one of the design flaws of online learning. So, designing in places in your course when you establish yourself as the audience for their writing can help mitigate this uncertainty for students.

Identifying how you will "frame" yourself is part of determining how responsive you will be and what kind of feedback you'll provide on the various assignments, from their discussion boards, and peer review activities, to their longer research-based projects. In face-to-face courses, the question of audience is sometimes a challenge for students, but in online courses, this challenge is multiplied because of the lack of face-to-face contact between student and instructor, therefore it is imperative to "establish yourself appropriately as an audience" to help students understand how to situate the work they are doing for your course (Warnock, 2009, p. 1). As the instructor, you are one audience students are targeting, but you must work even harder to get students to understand how to compose a text for the audience an assignment requires.

The design of your course offers a lot of opportunity to get students to understand composing for audience. You can have your students participate in activities where you and the other students in the course act as audience, or you can have your students pair off and use each other as the audience on a specific writing assignment (like writing letters back and forth about a topic or issue). Alternatively, you can build in more of the smaller/shorter writing assignments where you give the students an opportunity to test you out as a reading audience (the discussion boards are great for this!). Warnock (2009) offers some more good advice about the smaller assignment opportunities. He states that though the job of an online instructor requires a lot of interaction and response, "Luckily, in this environment, you don't *need* to comment on every post, because students do much of that work for you . . . Let the students roam. Let them sustain the conversation with questions and comments" (2009, p. 76). Good advice when you think about the design of your online course. Build in those places where you can practice audience and audience awareness without having to respond to every thing every student says.

You're probably sitting there going, "yea, well all this is great but this is going to take so much time!" Believe us, we get it. Teaching online is a huge time commitment. As we said earlier in the book, teaching online requires more than just putting your face-to-face class materials in the CMS. Hewett (2015) discusses the challenge of time for online instructors, "Time is a huge issue for OWI instructors—both teachers and tutors—and we are rightly concerned whenever something, including a new response approach, threatens to cause us to expend more time . . . It seems important to recognize consciously, though, that such a decrease in teaching is caused directly by the teaching load rather than the text-rich literacy load of OWI" (pp. 205–206). To address expectations of the course and to offer students clear guidelines for instructor response time in various areas of the course, and to address the type of feedback students can expect, some suggest laying groundwork at the beginning of the course through the use of introductory phone chats (conference call style) with three to four students and offering follow up synchronous chats throughout the term (Girardi, 2016, p.64). Hewett (2010) states "When essay response is an instructor's primary contribution to either an ongoing or one-time conversation about writing *and* when that conversation and its attendant teaching occurs entirely online, message clarity seems more crucial, particularly in pedagogies that value dialogue" (p.71). Dialogue, with audience and time, gives you an opportunity to be precise with your responses and makes you a better guide for the course. By being responsive with your design of your online writing course, you create an engaging space that is open to questions and comments from students who will be motivated to interact with the texts and their peers. And by learning where to comment and when to respond will save your energy for the duration of the class so you can be at your best to help your students learn to write and respond.

Responsive Instruction

One thing that new instructors often forget when teaching an online course is the value of balance. It's easy to get caught up in being present and trying to support students so much that you spend more time in the LMS than you would in a traditional face-to-face class. Warnock (2009) complicates this notion by stating, "Although you should be involved, the level of that involvement differs, both among teachers from conversation to conversation in a particular class . . . One of the tough parts of conducting [online] conversations is that you must participate in the conversation but resist the urge of being constantly drawn into discussions when they are irresistibly good—which, I warn you, happens often" (pp. 75–76). It is impossible to ask instructors to be available 24/7 when it comes to online writing classes. And before you say, "Well I do it when I teach face-to-face." Think about that. Do you? Do you *really*? In fact, this cannot be achieved in a face-to-face environment, so to suggest it can be created online is a disservice to students and instructors.

What we can do, as educators, is to promote a sense of a Return On Investment (ROI) time. Conrad and Donaldson (2012) note that, "An effective online instructor determines appropriate communication strategies, manages time demands, defines her or his evolving role as an online instructor, and establishes a presence within the online classroom" (p. 13). As Conrad and Donaldson suggest your role as an online instructor is ever evolving and one thing we've found that is a key part of this evolution is modeling. Modeling behavior in a digital space for your students is a great way to effectively use your time as an online instructor. Modeling also helps to create a responsive presence with your students. Modeling expectations is one of the first things instructors should do. You can model expectations in the announcements, the discussion boards, by posting sample student assignments, by talking with students via a video in which you talk about your expectations, etc. Many students enter online courses thinking that they are work at your own pace correspondence-type courses and so it's important to set clear expectations for their responses as well as your own.

Responsive instruction helps to break this correspondence-course mentality because it shows you're in the course and you're with them helping them be successful along the way. It also illustrates that the course is more than a transactional space. That one can go in and out of the online space just as one goes in and out of the F2F classroom. Presence and space go hand in hand so when thinking about your responsiveness as an instructor and how much time you want to spend in the course. It's equally important that you also think about being away from the course. Space in online courses is imperative and being mindful to take advantage of the spaces in an online course can actually prove to be rewarding: ". . . online courses involve greater distance gaps and fewer physical cues (facial and other visual representations of emotion, etc.), both of which can create gaps in understanding. While it is useful to identify, address, and mind the gaps in physical, virtual and cognitive spaces in online learning, we also need to spend some time exploring the productive nature of gaps as well" (Carter & Rickly, 2005, p. 130). By making students feel like a priority and stipulating that you will return feedback and emails on various topics and assignments within a certain time frame, you can create a stable space where students know what to expect when it comes to your availability and their own. Setting up a schedule for returning feedback and grades within a class establishes a routine to help students know where they are in the class and where you are in terms of workload. This is more than just a work-life balance, this is about a work-teach-learn balance that is needed for you and your students to be successful in an online space.

Warnock (2015) adds to this notion of space and presence when he suggests that instructors create space from the start of a course in order to create expectations of responsiveness for students that the allow the instructor to disconnect and reconnect: "Whether OWI teachers provide response windows or give students timing expectations in days or hours, they should create an understanding of expectations of how issues might be resolved . . . Doing so builds appropriate boundaries, trust, and a sense of relationship'" (p. 167). Hewett (2010) adds to this noting,

> Students also learn to trust their instructors by knowing what teachers/tutors expect from them . . . Students need to know whether they can contact an instructor whenever the platform

makes them aware of the instructor's presence in the online classroom or tutorial setting. If there are restrictions, like the need for an appointment or to honor certain office hours, students should be told when an instructor welcomes such contact. (p. 47)

When you teach face-to-face and you go over the syllabus with your students on the first day, you might say that the document is a contract between you and the students that hold them accountable for behavior in the class, assignments, workload, and so on. For an online course, this is also important for you as the instructor so you are held responsible for being responsive and on time. Don't ask your students to do something you are incapable of doing.

Establishing a routine for your feedback and responses should echo the schedule. Students who meet online have lives like you, but if they know the schedule, they can understand when and how you are responding to their feedback. In Figure 3.1 is a typical week for Casey's summer writing class (normally a project like this would happen over four weeks, but in summer he is dealing with ⅓ of the time). This is not an ideal timeline as it condenses so much, but each week runs the same in terms of when the project is assigned, when student feedback is due (yours as well!), when the revision plan is due, and when the final draft is due.

Monday	Tuesday	Wednesday	Thursday	Friday	Saturday	Sunday
Project #1 sent out -work on draft	Work on draft	Submit to Eli Review for Peer Review Feedback	Peer Review	Peer Review due You (instructor) respond	Revision Plan due You (instructor) respond to Plan	Final draft due You (instructor) respond to final drafts next day

Figure 3.1

Being on this type of schedule helps both you and your students. You know when they have things due for you and when you have things due for them. It keeps the semester in a rhythm that is admittedly fast paced, but it also controls when and how you respond. While you may see this scheduling as one more thing to do, another time commitment, we promise this effort will be worth it and will go a long way in helping you keep your sanity. Here are a few strategies from experts on how to deal with the scheduling and time allocations of online courses:

• Being Organized
• Being Disciplined

- Distinguishing Between Work and Personal Life
- Being Flexible (Lehman & Conceicao, 2011, pp. 91–93)

Additional suggestions include:

- Remember to make time to care for yourself
- Establish priorities and remember it's not necessary to respond to every-one at once
- Ask students to keep email to a minimum (post questions in the class-room instead)
- Establish agreement as to the nature of postings in online discussions
- Delegate work to students (Bender, 2012, p. 156).

While these are all good suggestions, we've found in our experience you need a little trial and error to find what works best for you. We do feel that being or-ganized and having a clear purpose/strategy can help with the time suck that can be challenging for online writing instructors. It's so easy to get overly involved in your course which is why discipline is listed above as one strategy to combat this pull from the online courses you teach. We know as writing instructors that we can sometimes get caught up in giving feedback on students' writing, so much so that it becomes overwhelming for students. The same can be said for online courses, you can be too present and provide too many comments in the discus-sion areas, post too many announcements and be too available to your students so utilize the above strategies to help you.

Another component of responsive instruction occurs in the feedback you give students on their writing assignments. Part of this individualized teaching includes building a relationship with each individual student in your course. Stu-dents need to build a relationship of trust with you as their instructor because they are sharing something very personal with you: their writing. Get to know your students by responding to their writing and to them as students, not just users in the class taking it for a grade. A high level of communication is one consideration for ensuring course success and responding to student writing is one of the most apparent opportunities for building up the communication lines between instructor and student (Conrad & Donaldson, 2012). Additionally, as we all know, "the feedback from teachers is one thing that students count on as cru-cial to their learning" (Hewett, 2015, p. 190). But we and others see the feedback on student writing to be even more important in an online setting because "[r]es-ponding to students is crucial teaching work because feedback provides students with their most individualized teaching experience in online settings" (Warnock, 2015, p. 166). Some like to provide audio or audio/video feedback, and providing written feedback on writing is still an option that many online instructors utilize, but due to the context of the online environment, it's important that you are in-credibly clear and that your tone is upbeat and encouraging.

Additionally building weekly or semi-weekly feedback check-ins with each student about their writing in whatever format works for you helps with the rapport building that Glaizer (2016) and others stress as a key to persistence in online courses, "Building rapport is really about building relationships—and that is not done in a single shot . . . Similarly, rapport building should not be a superficial effort" (p. 5). We think instructors need to develop a responsive strategy as to *how* they give feedback on students' written work. Students can't hear the tone of your voice or see your body language and eye contact like they would in a face-to-face student/instructor conference, so it's imperative that you proofread, edit, and revise your written feedback for clarity, "Given this reading load [2.75 times greater than a F2F course], a teacher's incomplete or underdeveloped thought in an email or discussion post can lead to multiple problems of student comprehension and teacher *ethos*. Instructors must carefully proofread their own work for content and clarity; this work places them in the role of *modeling* communication behavior and *strong writing skills* . . ." (Warnock, 2015, p. 157). Developing instructor *ethos* is a key to success as an online instructor, so we suggest the following advice when giving feedback on student writing:

- Be clear and concise—tie in your feedback with the objectives of assignment.
  - ▷ Maybe even have some standard feedback ready and waiting that you have prepared ahead of time that you know will work for online feedback.

- Use a conversational tone, as if the student were in your office and you were walking them through your comments and their paper.
  - ▷ We like to start feedback off with, "Hi Karen, looks like you are off to a good start. If you notice in the first paragraph . . ."

- Include links to examples you reference—the course is online, so take advantage of the medium.
  - ▷ Make sure the links you share are accessible and ADA compliant— not all students have access to every site.

- Make video or sound recordings so students can hear your voice accompanied with your written feedback. Even if you only do this once at the beginning of the semester, they will hear your tone and voice and apply it to all written feedback going forward.
  - ▷ If you make a video, be sure to close caption it, and if you do only sound, make sure you also give students a script.

- Reference discussion posts or other writings from students in the class that have shared their texts with the course to build the peer-to-peer learning space.
  - ▷ Your students are an amazing resource! Help them help each other!

- Make a screencast of you going over feedback students give each other (remove the names) so you can talk about what good feedback is. This can also give you a good idea of whether or not the students understand the assignment.
  ▷ Again, close caption the video so it is accessible.

We know that these are only a few, but by trying some of these helped us to better communicate with our students about what the course is about and also conveyed how much we cared about their growth as writers.

In addition to building the relationship and nurturing the communication lines with your students you also want to reduce their stress by communicating with them effectively in regards to how quickly you'll respond to their written work. We noted this above but we can't stress it enough! Communicating response time can reduce students' anxiety and help them feel more at ease while awaiting your feedback. Further, communicating response times helps the instructor set realistic expectations, human expectations, for how quickly he/she will respond because it's easy to get sucked into instant thinking (the course is online so everything must happen instantaneously!). "One reason for establishing feedback timing is to aid students in their writing and planning, but another important reason is for the teachers' benefit. OWI teachers do not want students to have unreasonable (maybe on a human endurance level) expectations of response" (Warnock, 2015, pp. 166–167). As seasoned online writing instructors, we know how hard it is to limit yourself or cut back on trying to anticipate and solve problems before they happen, so it can be just as challenging to set limits with yourself as it is to set limits with your students. We also know from experience that students can be aware when you're not fully engaged and if you respond too quickly with unclear comments or feedback that is too vague. Being responsive in your instruction is about working **with** your students, not **against** them.

Responsive Administration

Being a responsive administrator is not just about sitting around and waiting for faculty contact, it is also about answering and returning small email queries about assignments and scheduling. Being responsive is supporting students and faculty, even when they cannot see you. It is about setting up a schedule that works to minimize miscommunication. Being a responsive administrator means responding to faculty when problems arise and getting your faculty what they need in terms of skills and resources before problems arise. Just as a teacher would respond to a student who had questions and concerns about a class, as the administrator, you must respond to the needs of your faculty. This does not mean that you are available 24/7, but it does mean that you are ready to help faculty get the skills and resources they need. You have to understand that just because your online classes may be accessible 24/7, that does not meet you or your faculty should be. Casey has caught himself sending emails at crazy hours assuming a faculty member is awake—he used to be like his students who said they emailed him a few minutes ago and were patiently awaiting a response! As an administrator, you want to be supportive, not presumptuous and exploitive of faculty time.

Admins also need to provide excellent professional development opportunities for faculty to improve their many skills. These opportunities can be seen as attending workshops across campus or having guest speakers come to your department to discuss distance education. Casey sets up these opportunities so faculty can put these lines in their CVs and write about their experiences for the review process. At MSU, there is a healthy population of faculty and staff who teach and research distance education—multiple lunches and workshops on new pedagogies are available for faculty who teach online from departments all over campus. There are also workshops and tutorials for how to use various course management systems like Desire2Learn, Google Sites, Google Classroom, and others. These types of workshops are helpful for faculty to update their skills on various platforms that are free to the university—these are also platforms that students are familiar with from working with them in other courses. If there are no workshops available, see if you can bring in guest speakers from nearby universities that have strong distance education programs to present their best practices to faculty, answer questions, and even set up a workshop for the entire campus (we recommend the entire campus because you might get more funding for the speaker and workshops if you make it available to all faculty). You can also have presenters via video-conference and ask them to discuss new and exciting opportunities with distance education—this will also put the presentation online so anyone can attend and you can record it so faculty who couldn't make it can access it later.

Your faculty are an asset! Samantha Bernstein and Adrianna Kezar (2016) make an excellent observation about the perception and role of non-tenure (NT) faculty in the university:

> For example, unlike tenure-track faculty, contingent faculty have little or no involvement in curriculum planning or university governance, little or no access to professional development, mentoring, orientations, evaluation, campus resources or administrative support; and they are often unaware of institutional goals and outcomes. (para. 19)

Invite all of your faculty to contribute. Invite tenure and non-tenure faculty to be a part of the conversation. Casey has been pretty lucky to be at MSU where NT faculty are engaged in lots of service via search committees, advisory councils, merit review committees, and college and university level committees that are a great way for all faculty to see how the university works. We also believe you need to involve NT faculty in your curriculum committee. What are your program's learning outcomes? What are your learning goals? Being responsive is also about responding to the needs of your program. It is about being aware of the amazing skills and talents of your NT faculty in a way that supports their careers and enriches the experiences of your students. As an administrator, you are doing more than just scheduling. It's not about making faculty and students happy, it's about everything you do that supports their efforts to improve as colleagues and as students to be successful in and beyond the university.

If you do this, then faculty will also acquire new skills that they can also apply to new software and hardware. We talked about using software to make videos for online classes in the personal section of this book, so making sure faculty have access to such software like Camtasia or Quicktime so they can make their own videos is essential. Software includes video conferencing like Skype, Google Hangouts, or Zoom. If your university has a deal in place with Zoom or Microsoft, they might also have workshops or tech support for the software—it would be a great thing to have someone from tech support come to your program and work with your faculty to solve problems before they arise. If they don't have such support, dig through the mountains of videos online that can help. And if you can't find any, as you become more proficient from using the software on your own, make your own videos and help educate and support your faculty. We both have made countless how-to videos for a variety of software and websites because we couldn't find what we wanted.

Hardware is also important when it comes to teaching online. You will need to make sure that faculty have up-to-date technology to make videos, hold video conferences, upload large video files, and enough storage to hold them. Larger hard drives can help backup whatever content faculty store in the cloud like courses and large video files. A good camera and microphone can help faculty make clearer videos that allow greater understanding of text being spoken in the videos. With better cameras and recording equipment comes better quality and better accessibility for students. See if there are recording studios on campus or nearby where your department can book time for faculty to record and make videos for students. Build up a library of videos used in previous online courses so new faculty can get an idea of what they can do, how to do it, and why it is so important. If someone in your program is amazing at some of these things, incentivize their cooperation and willingness to help. As the administrator, you must support your faculty, and in doing so, support students. Responsiveness as an administrator can take on a lot of different forms but the most consistent form is how you respond to your instructors to make them feel like they are not alone.

As we've stressed a lot in our sections on administration, you must find ways to support your online writing instructors. Responsive administration is very similar to responsive instruction but your audience is your group of instructors instead of students. Much of what we said about responsive instruction can be applied to administration. Creating a practice for how you'll respond to your instructors is just as imperative as creating a practice for how you'll respond to your students. You can't be all things and be available all the time for your instructors. Therefore, you'll want to teach them some self-sufficiency and provide them with a list of university resources they can access when they can't access you. We also have found that supporting instructors can look very different at different institutions so it's best to create a strategy for responding to your instructors' needs that works for your institution. For example, some institutions have robust training and resources for people who are new to online teaching but other institutions have zero training and very limited resources (usually just resources on how to use the CMS) so figure out what your institution has so that you can determine what resources you can rely on that are already available and what resources you'll need to make in order to have an arsenal of pre-made videos (as noted above). And of course, we highly recommend you send new online instructors to The Online Writing Instruction Community (www.owicommunity.org). We're big on not reinventing the wheel and we suggest you take on that mentality too since we all know how overloaded administration jobs can become.

Final Thoughts

The goal of being responsive is to help you maintain a high level of interaction with your students while not getting buried under the avalanche of emails and essays. It's about finding a balance—a good understanding of how an online course works so you can teach students. Just as you would get breaks between classes for breakfast, lunch, and dinner, schedule these into your calendar and make sure you are still you while teaching. We know this sounds obvious, but you will be surprised how checking your email can dominate your day. Remember, you won't see them in class on Monday or Tuesday or any day of the week, but you will see them via email, through their discussion posts, through assignments they turn in, or through a scheduled video conference. If you host office hours with a digital conference space that is open for any student to log in, schedule some writing time or grading time during these hours just in case no one shows up. We have a friend who hosts online office hours with his computer camera pointed to a sign that says: "Hey, it's too nice for us to sit inside today. If you are online and want to talk, text me at this number ###-###-#### and I'll be back in less than a minute!" You can still be responsive to students without being online all the time.

For the Hole in One!

If there is one thing to take away from this chapter that is planning a responsiveness strategy for your administrative style, course design, and instruction is essential for success as an online instructor or administrator. We hope you see that you need to set expectations with your students and faculty in order to create a process of response that is doable and works for you in the long run. So, create a schedule that works for you and stick to it! In addition to planning out time to assess and respond to your students, you also need to plan out time for office hours and to answer emails. Further, if you design your own courses, you'll also need to schedule some time to work on improving or making changes to your course(s). However, you also need to consider planning and scheduling out time that you're not going to work; an essential step that most new online instructors miss. Scheduling downtime, professional development time, exercise time, mental health time, etc., is just as important as scheduling time to respond in the discussion boards or to comment on your students' essays.

For more practice and application examples, please visit our site: www. owicommunity.org.

Drive for Show, Putt for Dough!

Being available—The Master Scheduler!

(Casey)

Part of working with students in courses that can last anywhere from 6 to 16 weeks is that we be responsive to them. We have been fortunate to see a number of approaches with concern for not over-extending your availability—by that we mean being responsive without being on call. This is also important in terms of location as not all of your students may reside in the same time zone as you do or even in the same country.

Set the time zone for your class when it comes to due dates. Create the course schedule in your Course Management System (CMS) and stipulate certain hours that you will be online (morning for students who are well ahead of you in terms of a time zone and in the afternoon for students who may be behind you) so everyone has an opportunity to utilize your availability.

Below is a sample of what my normal day may look like while teaching in my summer six-week course. Schedule it the way you would if you were on campus and had face-to-face office hours and meetings. This establishes a routine for you and your students. When they see the times you are free, they have the opportunity to plan their schedules as well so they can set aside time to meet with you. This is not just about making yourself responsive, it is also about being open and personal. The PARS approach is built to overlap as each supports the other. As you do this, you build a stronger pedagogy and a digital, personal, and accessible bridge to your students.

Different colors afford me the opportunity to plan my day so I know when I have video conferences, when I need to work with my other computer for video production, set aside time for my own writing, and create time for me to respond to student writing, reviews in Eli Review, and student feedback.

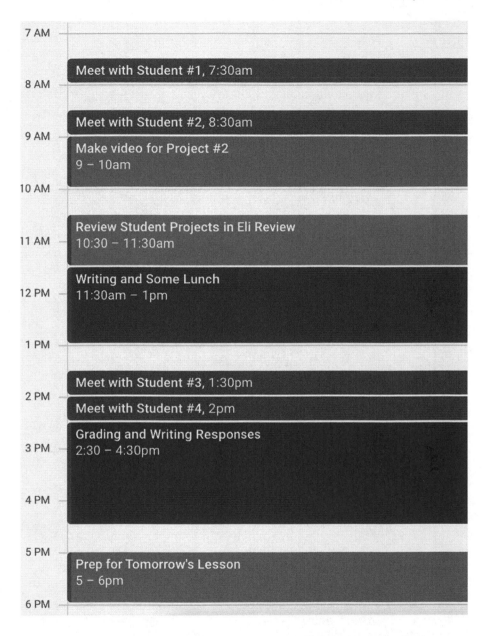

7 AM	
	Meet with Student #1, 7:30am
8 AM	
	Meet with Student #2, 8:30am
9 AM	Make video for Project #2 9 – 10am
10 AM	
11 AM	Review Student Projects in Eli Review 10:30 – 11:30am
	Writing and Some Lunch 11:30am – 1pm
12 PM	
1 PM	
2 PM	Meet with Student #3, 1:30pm
	Meet with Student #4, 2pm
3 PM	Grading and Writing Responses 2:30 – 4:30pm
4 PM	
5 PM	
	Prep for Tomorrow's Lesson 5 – 6pm
6 PM	

I organize my schedule the same way I do when I have face-to-face days on campus. Being responsive is one of the key steps in reaching students. I have far too many examples of evaluations where students noted how the schedule helped them to stay on task, how my emails were prompt and strategic, and how surprised they were that I was personal and responsive. By being a master scheduler, you can create an open and accessible space that allows for student success.

Figuring Out a Plan: If at first you don't succeed . . . keep working at it!
(Jessie)

I'll admit it. I'm really not good at working from home, like seriously, not good at all. I have little skill for managing time, and setting boundaries/expectations with my students. I am the instructor who's always checking her email (like 20 plus times a day!), the instructor trying to head off problems before they escalate, the instructor who wants to be über supportive for her students because she knows the challenges of feeling alone when taking a course online.

In reality, students probably like me a lot because I respond to their queries so quickly and I get them the help they need with little delay. However, my constant availability is not healthy; it's a sickness. I'm the always responsive and available online instructor, but recently, I've been trying to mend my evil ways.

I have spent the last ten+ years teaching online and I am just starting to get to a point where I have a regular schedule; I've failed multiple times trying to come up with something that works. The sheer number of planners, planning systems and calendars that I've gone through in the last few years, proves that it takes time to find out how to manage it all and with practice, you can get a system that works for you.

My latest quest to master my schedule is inspired by the fact that I'm burnt out, running on zero, have no energy left. I can't keep up the pace I've set anymore. I'm starting to realize that a schedule = freedom.

I've been working on prioritizing and I've been trying to pick the top three things that would make me feel like I had a good day, and that I was productive. I set aside time in my morning (during or after breakfast) to plan out my day and pick my top three priorities for the day. I also have begun meshing my personal schedule with my work schedule, which is helping. In the past, I've always kept these separate, but now I schedule out meetings for work, tasks for work, time to write professionally, exercise, do the laundry, etc., all in one place.

Every single day I fill out a schedule (yes, by hand!) that looks something like the following figure:

This is what works for me, but it wouldn't work for everyone. Developing a system takes time and skill. I've only been really working on it in the last year. Prior, I wasn't managing my workload or giving students a realistic idea of what it means to take a class online. While all of the experts say it's important to set a schedule, I was just putting one foot in front of the other and dealing with the day-to-day ebbs and flows that come with online teaching.

In finding your own unique schedule, I encourage you to experiment and figure out what kind of system you want to use:

- Will you do research on being productive or setting up a daily routine?
- Will you assess your current process and figure out what is working and what is not?

- Will your schedule be electronic or paper-based?
- Will you put both work and personal items in your schedule?
- Will you plan it out daily, weekly, monthly?
- Will you share it with others, like your family members?

Three Priorities:

1. workout
2. respond to student essays
3. work on C&C article

Daily Mind Dump

- Exercise
- Grade wk. 2 DQs
- House chores
- Respond to student essays
- Email about PARS book
- Participate in Week 3 DQs
- Laundry
- Walk dogs 2 times
- Work on C&C article
- Prep. dinner

6-8 a.m.	Breakfast, Walk dogs, House chores
8-10 a.m.	Work on C&C article, start laundry
10-11 a.m.	Email, course questions, grade wk. 2 DQs
11 a.m.-1 p.m.	Workout, lunch, shower
1-3 p.m.	Respond to student essays
3-5 p.m.	Grocery, dinner prep, continue laundry
5-7 p.m.	Dinner, house chores, veg out time
7-9	Email, walk dogs, bed

Considering these things and more is a great way to start to work on finding a system that works for you. I encourage you to do this sooner, rather than later. I would hope that you don't just jump into online teaching full force and start creating bad habits and unrealistic expectations for yourself and your students.

My advice: Don't wait nine+ years to realize what you've been doing isn't working. Start figuring out a plan today!

References

Bernstein, S. & Kezar, A. (2016). Is it time to eliminate tenure for professors? The Conversation. Retrieved from https://theconversation.com/is-it-time-to -eliminate-tenure-for-professors-59959.

Brown, B. (2018). *Dare to lead.* New York: Penguin Random House.

Carter, J. L. & Rickly, R. (2005). Mind the gap(s): Modeling space in online education. In K. Cargile Cook & K. Grant-Davie (Eds.), *Online education: Global questions, local answers* (pp. 123–139). Amityville, NY: Baywood Publishing Company.

Conrad, R. & Donaldson, J. A. (2012). *Continuing to engage the online learner: More activities and resources for creative instruction.* San Francisco: Jossey-Bass.

Glazier, R. (2016). Building rapport to improve retention and success in online classes. *Journal of Political Science Education, 12*(4), 437–456. doi:10.1080/15512169 .2016.1155994.

Hewett, B. (2010). *The online writing conference: A guide for teachers and tutors.* Portsmouth, NH: Heinemann.

Hewett, B. (2015). *Reading to learn and writing to teach: Literacy strategies for online writing instruction.* Boston: Bedford St. Martin's.

Warnock, S. (2009). *Teaching writing online: How & why.* Urbana, IL: NCTE.

Warnock, S. (2015). Teaching the OWI course. In B. Hewett & K. DePew (Eds.), *Foundational practices of online writing instruction* (pp. 151–181). Fort Collins, CO: The WAC Clearinghouse and Parlor Press. Retrieved from https://wac.colo state.edu/books/perspectives/owi/.

Chapter 4: Strategic

On the Tee! The **S** in PARS stands for **Strategic**. We feel that strategy is a pillar to success in distance education. The most important thing a (novice or experienced) instructor or administrator can do is be strategic about their process. Strategy is the key to the success or failure of an online course. If you take one thing from our entire book, we hope it is that you *must* have a strategy for the administration, instruction and design of your online writing courses!

Strategic OWI: Theory, Practice, and Significance to OWI

So much of online instruction is about strategy. We strongly believe that distance education could benefit from a stronger focus on strategy but not just any strategy, a strategy focused on the user experience of the students. Both of us have had terrible experiences in online courses and conferences (both teaching and taking). We can remember a time when we were participating in an online conference and we were both asked to be involved in developing and facilitating this conference. We experienced so much frustration during the process because no one had taken any time to develop a strategy for how the conference sessions would be given or how participants would get information on how to join the conference. Had there been a strategy in place that identified the target audience of the conference, what their needs/desires were for the sessions, and how the logistics were going to play out that the entire experience would've been better for everyone involved. This experience was an isolated one, but we feel that the reason this was a problem, as with so many of our experiences with online events, is due to lack of planning and strategizing the experience. Whether you're designing an online web conference or an entire online writing course, you must spend time on the front end creating a strategy.

Strategic Design

When planning the content of an online writing course, it's important to be strategic in your course design. We encourage you to think about it like this: you're creating a user experience for your students (the users) and you need to consider/plan for all of the elements of this experience in order to make it successful. It helps to plan out the entire semester, whether or not you share the whole semester layout with your students. Make a semester map where you write out everything you want the students to do and how these activities and assignments connect with the learning objectives for the course. It's best to work backwards from the larger assignments and then fill in the rest. The main thing to consider when creating a course design is who are your student users. How will they be accessing the content? How comfortable are they with technology? What do they need to learn to move on to the next course? Considering larger questions like these will help you map out a successful course design.

There is a lot of research done on strategic course design and there are a lot of best practices out there to ensure your design is accessible to students. We tend to apply user-centered practices to our online courses because we too feel that, "In user-centered learning, the focus is not on what is being taught but rather on how students are being engaged. A user-centered mindset returns students to the center of the conversation, energizing and improving professional development in which teachers and students, not technology, shape learning experiences" (Greer & Harris, 2018, p. 23). We also know from experience that being strategic up front with our online courses yields better results the rest of the semester. We know some best practices are useful, such as "OWI teachers should employ redundancy in their OWCs in the content, instructional texts, and any documents students must read or ideas that are crucial to their writing growth" (Warnock, 2015, p. 161) but we feel that other best practices those of user-centered design can be useful. Approaching the online course in a way that makes you think about designing an entire experience for a very specific user is a way to strategize.

Designing your online course should be a process and it takes time to figure out your own individual process and what works. Because both of us have been teaching both face-to-face and online for a number of years now we've honed our own personal processes and we've found ways to integrate user research into our courses in order to keep our students moving forward in the course material and in their progress as writers. The online course environment has multiple moving parts. Potts and Salvo (2017) argue that "Experience architecture requires that we understand ecosystems of activity rather than simply considering single task scenarios" (p. 4). Online writing courses are these complex ecosystems of activity, and user-experience design principles should be utilized to develop a more personalized view of learners' experiences and needs.

Potts and Salvo (2017) further argue that "To understand these ecosystems, we must move beyond isolated tasks of writing, designing, and programming. We need to gain a stronger understanding of strategy and be willing to lead initiatives in the name of the participants who will use these systems and the organizations that want to engage users as contributors" (p. 5). We agree that strategy is one answer to the dilemma of engaging students in their own online course experience. In online courses, the instructor is responsible for architecting an experience for the student users in a very specific environment (an LMS or CMS) but the online instructional design experience is foreign to many instructors. Many instructors are thrown into online teaching, which requires a lot of strategy and planning to be successful, luxuries that require time, something many do not have. To further complicate things, elements of face-to-face courses can rarely be successfully migrated into online ones. We feel that many instructors lack a strategy and skill set to understand and design for their student users.

Borgman and Dockter (2018) offer the following strategies to address accessibility and focus on the user when designing online courses:

- Soliciting student feedback on the course and course design early
- Utilizing student feedback in course design and operations
- Present content in multiple ways; utilize various learning methods
- Build in repetition of content throughout the course; scaffold learning
- Include captions on videos and offer transcripts
- Use structured (built-in) headings in Word documents and PDFs
- Include alternative text to describe images used in the class.
- Work with the university's accessibility office to ensure content is able to be accessed by all students
- Attend accessibility trainings/webinars when offered
- Frequently visit this site: https://www.usability.gov/what-and-why/user -centered-design.html (Borgman & Dockter, 2018, pp. 102–103).

Strategic Instruction

Most online instructors want to make "a real impact" on their students and being communicative is one of the best ways to help students understand what is expected and what they can expect from you, the instructor. Girardi (2016) argues that one of the reasons for frustration is because student and instructor expectations rarely align completely,

> Quite often, the expectations were that online courses should somehow be simpler than F2F courses, and online learners were supposed to learn my course was significantly challenging. Therefore, a potential cause of student disappointment and attrition is a lack of alignment between expectations and experience, both for the instructor and the students in a given course. To combat this, I suggest an honest discussion to discover, reveal and share expectations in the first week of the course. (pp. 72–73)

In other words, often a lot of the headaches that occur in online courses happen because of the gap in understanding of what is expected from each party involved, instructor and student. Setting up expectations through a myriad of ways (announcements, video, audio, phone chats, IM chats, email communication, etc.) is a great first step in helping students understand how you'll act and how they're expected to act in the digital space you share. Strategizing your instruction is essential. We can't stress this enough.

There are so many elements of being a strategic instructor and we discussed many of these in previous chapters but as a reminder these include: responding to students in the discussion forums, responding to student writing, responding to daily student communication, such as posted questions or email. However, we also feel being a strategic instructor includes knowing who you're teaching, knowing your student users. The student demographic in higher education, especially in distance courses, looks much way different than it did 50 years ago. The National Center for Education Statistics (NCES) has reported a growing trend in older, non-traditional students noting that among part-timers, "some 55 percent were young adults, 24 percent were ages 25–34, and 21 percent were age 35 and older" (Characteristics of Postsecondary Students, para. 5). With older non-traditional students comprising a majority of the student population, challenges of mixed age classes and proper support for these working adult students becomes concerning. Knowing who your students are is a large part of strategy. You need to design for these students. For example, the NCES indicates in recent years the trend of non-traditional student enrollment will continue and that by 2022–2023, the increase of students over 25 will be 20 percent (Cited in Olson, 2016, p. 130). This is true of both traditional face-to-face courses and online ones but many older students opt to take online courses or seek online degrees because of the flexibility it allows them to continue to work and support their families. So, if you know that most of your students will be older and will have packed schedules you can strategize your instruction to best suit their needs.

We have experienced mixed age student groups first hand in our own online writing courses. We're teaching students who are older than us. We're teaching students who are younger than us. We have classes that consist of 16- and 17-year-olds doing college transfer credit courses in high school and those same courses also include 40–50 year old students who are starting a new career. While research suggests that mixed-age courses, especially in digital environments, yields positive results, to get those results requires designing a program and its courses to support this diverse mix of learners (Olson, 2016, pp. 131–132). In addition to more older students, there is also a shift in minority attendance in secondary education. Joseph Williams (2014) reports that "Young people seeking higher education these days, they say, are less likely to be white or male, more likely to be Hispanic, may be the first person in their family to continue an education past high school, and will likely need help paying for it" (College of Tomorrow, para. 2). As economic data in the public sphere shows that people with college degrees do better financially, more and more students are returning to school to secure better employment. Again, knowing your students' motivations and possible distractions can help you put together a great student experience as you teach your course. If your students are older or don't have access to computers, you may, for example, need to build in a few lessons on how to use the technologies in your class, or you may need to build in more time for assignments so that the students can go to campus and use the campus computers to complete their assignments.

One of the challenges that this new student demographic brings to instructors is that now instructors need to work with varying degrees of skill level as well as varying degrees of English speaking and varying degrees of preparation for college level learning. Very often many of these returning students have been out of formal education for some time. Their skills as students have atrophied; what they remember from prior formal education courses might be forgotten. Thus, many students are entering college underprepared:

> . . . more than a third of all incoming college students are taking remedial classes, according to the 2012 NCES statistics, Latinos and African-Americans are more likely to need the extra help. Just over 41 percent of black freshmen need catch-up classes, compared to about 37 percent of Latinos and 31 percent of whites. (Williams, 2014, para. 18)

In addition to needing remedial courses, many students choose online courses because they mistakenly believe they'll be easier than going to campus. But online courses require time-management and computer skills that many returning students will need to learn, on top of the skills required to be a student again. Thus, when a college offers remedial courses or introductory courses online, the learning demand for these students is higher, causing higher dropout rates. Thinking about what level your students are at when they enter the course will determine the strategy you take in guiding them through the course assignments and the navigation of the course. You'll want to strategize your content to meet them where they are at, and trust us, from our experience, a lot of your students will be under-prepared. Many schools allow all students to take online courses whether or not they are suited to taking courses in a digital environment so you need to be prepared to work with this student demographic.

Instructors feel the challenge of dropout rates first-hand and we know from experience that instructors may feel very overwhelmed at times trying to "save" everyone in their course and help them be the best writers they can be. We have experienced countless challenges in facilitating a course with varying student skill and interest levels. We have taught many online courses at various levels and one of the biggest challenges we have seen has been working with are international students who go home for the summer. This is not a learning wall, but a functional wall we run into. Casey used to live in Google Docs as his CMS, but that doesn't work if just under half of his students reside in a country that denies access to Google. He can't ask his students to download a VPN to circumvent the laws of their nation, so he has to improvise and create alternative learning spaces for all students, not just a few. If he divided his content up for different sections of the class for different students, he denies them the learning space of interacting and providing feedback to one another, which is part of the learning process. To avoid this, he has to be strategic ahead of time so all students can access and contribute to the class. We know how challenging it can feel to be faced with an online course full of "newbies" but we also agree that "Online writing instruction as a discipline stands to benefit from a deeper engagement with the practices and mindset of user experience design because of the changing dynamics of our students" (Greer & Harris, 2018, p. 15). Instructors need to understand their users. Doing so will only help in lessening anxiety (of the instructor and student) about the online course experience.

One of the schools Jessie works for is a community college. This school has a varied student demographic. Some of the students taking her online 101 and 102 composition courses are taking them as high school students while others are in their mid-to-late 30s getting training to start a different career. There is also a high percentage of students who are first generation and minority. Many of the students attending this community college dropped out of high school and completed a G.E.D. or they completed high school but went directly into the workforce because they didn't like school. Knowing the types of students that she can have in her courses allows her to plan for the roadblocks to learning that might occur. It is important to avoid, "approaching the development of an online course based upon what design and teaching methods might be easiest and favored by the teacher [because this approach] is problematic and fails to consider the uniqueness of the students within the online course" (Borgman & Dockter, 2018, p. 103). One of the challenges that online instructors often face is strategizing the use of instructional tools and knowing who you're teaching helps you to successfully select the best tools available.

Strategic Administration

Digital technologies have changed the way we write and collaborate. As faculty, we now compose and design texts with technical skills and tools that did not exist when we were undergraduate students. We have learned to adapt our practices to these new tools. The same will happen for our students, who will greet new writing challenges with tools we can no more imagine now than the professors who taught us ten, twenty, or thirty years ago could imagine the technologies we use today. Many students are entering fields where not only writing skills, but also a vast range of composing and designing skills will be expected. As an administrator of a program, you must recognize that technology and workplace demands are going to drive the content of your program. Programs and faculty have an ethical imperative to design courses and pedagogies to meet the needs of the students they enroll and to meet the needs of increasingly diverse student populations. Working with diverse populations and varied reading audiences is a key skill that all workers must possess as Leijten, et al. (2014) remind us "Like most writing today—whether at school or in the workplace—professional writing takes place in a digital context . . . writing processes are now more than ever characterized by features of the digital workplace. [This] communication involves intense collaborations with others (both face-to-face and electronic) . . . These interactions involved constructing and reconstructing one's own and others' texts—refashion and reusing content from multiple sources" (p. 286). Students need to know how to communicate digitally in their workplaces and work across time zones/countries, and work with many different types of people.

As administrators, you need to strategize how you'll prepare your online instructors for the student demographic they'll face. Online courses and degrees have an appeal that reaches diverse students—the returning full-time working student with a family, the part-time student with a family, the military student stationed overseas, the former college student dropout who is returning to school after a large break spent working. In the most basic sense, we now teach anyone who has the desire to learn and the hope of an advanced degree (Friedman, 2018, 2017; Smith, 2014). Because of this massive shift to serving online students,

> [w]ith the rise of online learning in all forms, academia must continue to change with societal demands and student needs. Nonetheless, for the most part, the composition field's approach to teacher training has not evolved to include the pedagogies of online education, particularly that of teaching writing—regardless of genre—online. Rhetoric and Composition [as a field] needs to train GTAs [and others] to teach such composing—indeed, all writing—in online settings, including blended, hybrid, and fully online. (Bourelle, 2016, p. 91)

We agree with this sentiment and have both experienced this first hand. Neither of us had any formal online teaching training and both figured it out as we continued doing it. We both had teacher training in our master's programs but none that focused on writing in online environments such as online courses.

We find it difficult to deny the desire for more online courses with the recent explosion of EdX style massive online courses being added at universities across the country. What is true of student populations overall in higher education holds for online writing courses: "OWI students are adolescents entering college from high school, young adult students with a few years of work between high school and college, mature adults who tried college earlier and—for a wide range of reasons—stopped and decided to return later in life, and other adults whom college is a brand-new opportunity" (Hewett, 2015, p. 14). Distance education offers these students the best option to merge their home and work lives in pursuit of an advanced degree and beyond the appeal of flexibility, there are many other appeals to learning online, including the lack of travel time (a variety of learning spaces such as home, office, etc.), the convenience of asynchronous work (one can work at his/her own pace and time), the ability for students to focus course projects on topics relevant to their current job (applicable work), and several other benefits that are unique to each individual student. These demands have changed the way that writing programs handle their curriculum and the skills they attempt to teach in their writing courses. And these demands have spurred many students to return to school to support their workplace growth:

> Today's workplaces require you to understand and adapt to many communication challenges, such as global communication, cross-functional and cross-cultural teaming, fluctuating information environments and technologies, rapid writing assignments; short turnarounds or deadlines, and client development in project development and implementation. (Baehr & Cargile Cook, 2016, p. 1)

In many cases, these students are returning to finish a degree they started. In other cases, returning students want to improve existing skills and to learn the new skills their life and career requires for their personal and professional growth. These students often seek recognized programs that have a history of traditional, face-to-face graduates succeeding in their fields. Program administrators and instructors have to be flexible to changing demands brought on by technology and need to adapt writing courses to work in digital environments in order to teach transferable skills.

Having some industry experience gives us an excellent view of academic spaces that would normally be missed. We can't tell you how many meetings we've attended that could have been handled with an email or went 30 minutes too long. The administration of OWI faculty and students takes even more time as you are working in distributed groups. These groups might be scattered around the region, country, and even world. You have groups of faculty, groups of students, groups of staff, and groups of technical support. Think about the digital dance that has to happen to get all of these groups in tune so everyone can be on task.

The most important thing to do is create a plan. Casey has been the Associate Chair for Undergraduate Studies at Michigan State University where he has had to administer two programs, Professional and Public Writing and Experience Architecture—that's roughly 30 some faculty and around 300 students. Both programs average a total of eight online classes in the summer with each compressed into a six and a half week window that is normally 15 weeks. Working with faculty to get them prepared stems from a strategic plan that is created in early spring in preparation for the summer. Based on his experience he's created a quick checklist for you to go over as you get prepared to support your faculty:

1. Hardware
2. Software
3. Orientation
4. Support documents

First on the list is to find out what hardware your faculty might need. You do hardware first because it takes longer than software—software you can download, hardware not so much. Make sure your faculty have the hardware to successfully host and teach the class. Do they need webcams? Microphones? Headphones? A larger hard drive (internal or external) for video storage? Sent out this email to all faculty who are teaching online for the next cycle and ask for requests. Give yourself the time you need to meet their needs.

Second on the list is software or access to CMS or other online spaces. Do they need video editing software? Sound editing software? Video conferencing software? Do you need to pay for a subscription service they want to use like Eli Review? Get as many of these issues out of the way as soon as you can so you are doing more pedagogical support for your faculty in the summer than technical support.

Third on the list is having a small orientation with them online. We recommend Zoom because it operates at a low bandwidth, which means faculty who don't have access to reliable internet can use it and also call in. In this orientation you should guide them through specific goals you want them to meet for the teaching cycle they will be in. This list can vary from program to program, but be sure to cover assignments, accessibility issues, functional issues, and availability concerns. Casey always runs through his time management pitch when working with faculty and quick workarounds to various technologies. For example, he doesn't email students large files anymore. Depending on the systems in place at your school, he creates folders either in the CMS or in another cloud storage spaces and adds and removes files there. With only a few clicks he can share files with comments and grades rather than sending thirty separate emails to thirty separate students.

Fourth on the list is running your faculty through some support emails that mimic the PARS approach. Keeping several documents nearby you can send out at a moment's notice is ideal so faculty can get the help they need as soon as possible. What works for us is a good Google Doc that has links to recent articles on OWI pedagogy, campus resources, and help/tutorial videos on common problems you have found while teaching online. Casey has a long, but he believes a well-organized, Google Doc that acts like a check-list for faculty to go through when it comes to either answering technical problems or providing links on how to better use your Google Drive (as in, be more strategic with the tools you have so you don't have to try and learn an entirely new one within a few days!). You need to let your faculty know you are there for them, that you are available to help them, that you will respond as needed, and that you are strategic with your support, and that it is consistent.

Traditionally, admins establish the content and philosophy of a writing program. However, with the upsurge in courses moving from face-to-face to online, this can get lost. Administrators can be at a loss for who to assign the online writing courses he/she must offer. Oftentimes, these courses get assigned to faculty with little experience or interest in OWI and the administrator usually has little resources to provide professional development opportunities in OWI to the instructors assigned to teach the OWCs. There are a lot of ways that administrators can be strategic, from the planning and developing of OWCs, to the instructor assignments, assessment and evaluation practices used.

As we mentioned in the responsive chapter, many of the ideas we shared about being a strategic instructor can also be applied to being a strategic administrator. As you've seen from the examples above, there is a lot to think about when you administer a program with online writing courses. Not only are you just doing regular administration jobs but when your program has online courses, you're also in theory either becoming an instructional designer and/or helping your instructors become instructional designers or working together in some sort of team to take your face-to-face courses online with success. Therefore, strategy is a must. As the administrator you're going to want to create a strategy that helps you create the same quality online courses as you have face-to-face courses. You'll need a strategy to help you train and support the instructors who teach these courses and you'll need to figure out a strategy for how you're going to assess you instructors' teaching effectiveness in the online environment. Attempting to do any of this without a strategy will only result in disaster for the users (students and faculty) and you won't get the results you want either.

Final Thoughts

Distance education courses have literally changed the face of higher education. They've brought education to those that may have never even dreamed of a college degree. Designing, instructing and administering online writing courses have become a new focus of some writing programs but as we noted above this move to online requires a clearly thought out strategy that keeps the student users as the focus. It has become clear that

> [t]he institutional structure has shifted with the addition of online courses. These have materialized rapidly as a way to balance the budget, to offer great accessibility to college education and to solve classroom space concerns . . . Online education is the victim of its own success; it is the situation where a municipality builds a huge shopping mall, and then after the grand opening, the city sends a construction crew to widen the road that leads to the mall. (Mechenbier, 2015, p. 239)

Sadly, too many programs fail to offer the necessary professional development support faculty need. When combined with a lack of student support, it increases the likelihood that online and hybrid courses will become cycles of despair and dysfunction, where faculty blame underprepared students and students give up on poorly executed online courses. We've experienced this first hand at our own institutions and we've talked with a lot of our colleagues who have experienced it too.

We have seen a lot of schools across the country have be a victim of their own success because they've jumped on board, adding online courses and degrees, but failed to consider or better yet, plan for the various "roadblocks" to success (Mechenbier, 2015, p. 239). Or to borrow from Mechenbier's (2015) analogy, the support lanes haven't been added to the roads online learning relies on. Online learning requires two new crucial support lanes, one for students, one for faculty.

For students, many schools and departments fail to realize that if they're taking their courses online they need to provide online tutoring and writing support. Students need support for learning how to learn online, being prepared for the course's intellectual demands, and balancing life's demands with educational demands (DePew, 2015). For faculty, many programs fail to realize that teaching online, while rewarding, requires careful preparation and attention to practice. And it requires the professional development support, including the time necessary to help faculty redesign their face-to-face teaching practices for online environments. We know that this support is not always there, so we hope this book will help. Because of this huge influx of new distance education students, many schools are relying on contingent faculty to teach their online courses. Yet they offer them little to no training and due to their resilience, many contingent faculty "figure it out" and create successful online writing courses, but this happens with more extra work and headaches than would occur were professional development support made available.

Think about how strategic you are with your face-to-face courses. Think about how long you take to plan each day's lesson and activities. When you teach online, you also have to negotiate the digital space as well—your pedagogy may work face-to-face, but does it work solely online? Being strategic with your time and pedagogy will create a more viable learning space for students so you don't have to worry so much about functional issues and you can focus more on working with students so they can learn the topics related to the course. Think about the goals and learning outcomes of the course—how can being strategic help your students meet and exceed them?

For the Hole in One!

Planning is essential to being a successful online writing instructor or administrator.

Instructors:

Before the semester begins spend some time strategizing how it will go. Spending some time on the front end of teaching will save you time during the semester. With a little strategy you'll be able to carve out a plan for success.

- Plan out your assignments so that they're not all due at one time or due during a busy week in your personal life.
- Plan out your teaching. Where in the course can you best insert yourself as a teacher and make the most impact?
- Map out your instruction goals and how you're going to accomplish them.
- Review your course materials to ensure you're providing information through various channels and including all learning styles.
- Devise a strategy for making your presence known and connecting with the students so that they see you as a real live person and not just a computer.
- Reflect on the PARS elements and ensure you've addressed: being **Personal**, making you and your course materials **Accessible**, setting expectations for **Responsiveness** and creating a **Strategy** to help you and your students succeed.

Administrators:

Make an online teaching strategy survival guide for your online instructors. This could be a simple as listing out the weeks in the semester and indicating what instructors should be doing or focusing on, as shown in the following example.

For more practice and application examples, please visit our site: www. owicommunity.org.

Before the course begins	Email students to inform them that they are taking a distance education course
	Provide resources for the students on how to access the school's learning management system (LMS) and take the online trainings (if available) so that the students can prepare to navigate the LMS
	Inform students of the support systems available to distance students (tutoring hours, writing center, etc.)
Week 1	Email students a welcome email
	Participate in the introductory/ice breaker discussion
	Halfway through the week reach out to students who've not logged in yet
	Offer virtual office hours or meet and greet using a web conferencing platform like Zoom or GoTo Meeting
Week 2	Email students a welcome to Week 2 message and give them a preview of what's due that week
	Phone or email the students who didn't participate in Week 1
	Provide feedback on the assignments from Week 1
	Send out a reminder about the campus and online resources available
	Hold another virtual office hours session
Week 3	Email students a welcome to Week 3 message and give them a preview of what's due that week
	Contact the advisors for the students who aren't participating
	Provide feedback on the assignments from Week 2

And so on for the rest of the semester . . .

Drive for Show, Putt for Dough!

The following screenshot is for one of Casey's Eli Review summer writing classes. You can see all of the tasks are lined up like dominoes. All of these are linked in the syllabus and ready for the students to access and complete. It took a few hours to set up all of these tasks, upload the assignment text, insert peer review rubrics, and provide language and videos on what makes good feedback—but it is all worth it. As the semester moves on, students can see what is expected of them, when things are due, how they will be assessed on the assignment, and how they will be assessed on the peer review.

By being strategic with this schedule, it ensures that everyone will be on task for the duration of the classes and students, and instructors, will know what is expected of them. For an example, view the following figure.

Writing as Inquiry (WRA-101-■■■)

Home   Roster   Completion   Analytics   Downloads   Settings

Task Type	Task Name	Due Date ▾	Progress
Resubmit	Revision of Project #5 Direction Draft		93%
Revision	Revision Report for Project #5 Direction Draft		93%
Review	Project #5 Direction Draft Review		85%
Writing	Project #5 Direction Draft		93%
Resubmit	Revision of Outline for Project #5		93%
Revision	Revision Report for Outline for Project #5		93%
Review	Review of Outline for Project #5		82%
Writing	Outline for Project #5		93%
Resubmit	Revision of Project #4 Direction Draft		11%
Resubmit	Revision of Revision of Project #4 Direction Draft		0%
Revision	Revision Report for Revision of Project #4 Direction Draft		0%
Review	Project #4 Direction Draft Review		77%
Writing	Project #4 Direction Draft		89%
Resubmit	Revision of Outline for Project #4		85%
Revision	Revision Report for Outline for Project #4		85%
Review	Review of Outline for Project #4		86%
Writing	Outline for Project #4		96%
Resubmit	Revision of Project #3 Direction Draft		93%
Revision	Revision Report for Project #3 Direction Draft		94%
Review	Project #3 Direction Draft Review		86%
Writing	Project #3 Direction Draft		93%
Resubmit	Revision of Project #2 Direction Draft		100%
Review	Review of Interview Questions		99%
Review	Review of Outline for Project #3		88%
Revision	Revision Report for Project #2 Direction Draft		100%
Writing	Interview Questions		100%
Writing	Outline for Project #3		96%
Review	Project #2 Direction Draft Review		100%
Writing	Project #2 Direction Draft		100%
Resubmit	Revision of Outline for Project #2		100%
Revision	Revision Report for Outline for Project #2		100%
Review	Review of Outline for Project #2		100%
Writing	Outline for Project #2		100%
Resubmit	Revision of Project #1 Direction Draft		100%
Revision	Revision Report for Project #1 Direction Draft		100%
Review	Project #1 Direction Draft Review		100%
Writing	Project #1 Direction Draft		100%
Resubmit	Revision of Outline for Project #1		100%
Revision	Revision Report for Outline for Project #1		100%
Review	Review for Response to "The Importance of Feedback" (#FRC1)		100%
Review	Review of Outline for Project #1		100%
Writing	Outline for Project #1		100%
Writing	Respond to "Feedback and Improvement" (#FRC1)		100%

References

Bjork, C. (2018). Integrating usability testing with digital rhetoric in OWI. *Computers and Composition, 49*(2018), 4–13.

Borgman, J. & Dockter, J. (2018). Considerations of access and design in the online writing classroom. *Computers and Composition, 49*(2018), 94–105.

Bourelle, T. (2016). Preparing graduate students to teach online: Theoretical and pedagogical practices. *Writing Program Administration, 40*(1), 90–113.

Cargile Cook, K. (2005). An argument for pedagogy-driven online education. In K. Cargile Cook & K. Grant-Davie (Eds.), *Online education: Global questions, local answers* (pp. 49–66). Amityville, NY: Baywood Publishing Company.

Cook, K. C. (2007). Immersion in a digital pool: Training prospective online instructors in online environments. *Technical Communication Quarterly, 16*(1), 55–82.

Coombs, N. (2010). *Making online teaching accessible: Inclusive course design for students with disabilities.* San Francisco, CA: Jossey-Bass.

DePew, K. (2015). Preparing for the rhetoricity of OWI. In B. Hewett & K. DePew (Eds.), *Foundational practices of online writing instruction* (pp. 439–467). Fort Collins, CO: The WAC Clearinghouse and Parlor Press. Retrieved from https://wac.colostate.edu/books/perspectives/owi/.

Dutkiewicz, K., Holder, L. & Sneath, W. (2013). Creativity and consistency in online courses: Finding the appropriate balance. In K. Cargile Cook & K. Grant-Davie (Eds.), *Online education 2.0: Evolving, adapting and reinventing online technical communication* (pp. 45–72). Amityville, NY: Baywood Publishing Company.

Girardi, T. (2016). Lost in cyberspace: Addressing issues of student engagement in the online classroom community. In D. Ruefman & A. Scheg (Eds.), *Applied pedagogies: Strategies for online writing instruction* (pp. 59–74). Logan, UT: Utah State University Press.

Greer, M. & Harris, H. (2018). User-centered design as a foundation for effective online writing instruction. *Computers and Composition, 49*(2018), 18–24.

Hewett, B. & Ehmann Powers, C. (2004). *Preparing educators for online writing instruction: Principles and processes.* Urbana, IL: NCTE.

Johnson, S. & Berg, Z. (2012). Online education in the community college. *Community College Journal of Research and Practice, 36*(11), 897–902.

Meloncon, L. (2007). Exploring electronic landscapes: Technical communication, online learning, and instructor preparedness. *Technical Communication Quarterly, 16*(1), 31–53.

Meloncon, L. (2015). Preparing students for OWI. In B. Hewett & K. DePew (Eds.), *Foundational practices of online writing instruction* (pp. 411–438). Fort Collins, CO: The WAC Clearinghouse and Parlor Press. Retrieved from https://wac.colostate.edu/books/perspectives/owi/.

Minter, D. (2015). Administrative decisions for OWI. In B. Hewett & K. DePew (Eds.), *Foundational practices of online writing instruction* (pp. 211–225). Fort Collins, CO: The WAC Clearinghouse and Parlor Press. Retrieved from https://wac.colostate.edu/books/perspectives/owi/.

Nielsen, D. (2016). Can everybody read what's posted?: Accessibility in the online classroom. In D. Ruefman & A. Scheg (Eds.), *Applied pedagogies: Strategies for online writing instruction* (pp. 90–105). Logan, UT: Utah State University Press.

Potts, L. & Salvo, M. J. (2017). Introduction. In L. Potts & M. J. Salvo (Eds), *Rhetoric and experience architecture* (pp. 3–13). Anderson, SC: Parlor Press.

Smith, R. (2008). *Conquering the content: A step-by-step guide to online course design.* San Francisco: Jossey-Bass.

Snart, J. (2010). Hybrid learning: *The perils and promise of blending online and face-to-face instruction in higher education.* Santa Barbara, CA: Praeger Publishing.

Tobin, T., Mandernach, J. & Taylor, A. (2015). *Evaluating online teaching: Implementing best practices.* San Francisco: Jossey-Bass.

Warnock, S. (2009). *Teaching writing online: How & why. Urbana,* IL: NCTE.

Warnock, S. (2015). Teaching the OWI course. In B. Hewett & K. DePew (Eds.), *Foundational practices of online writing instruction* (pp. 151–181). Fort Collins, CO: The WAC Clearinghouse and Parlor Press. Retrieved from https://wac.colo state.edu/books/perspectives/owi/.

Conclusion

The 19th Hole!

Look to User Experience (UX) Research: Creating the Best Experience Possible for You and Your Students

As we conclude our text, we'd like to return to the golf metaphor that was the inspiration for the PARS approach. Golf is a game for life. You work to hone your golf game your entire life (or however long you play), but you never master the game; you never master the craft. Think about watching golf on TV or live (we do and we've heard the jokes, but stay with us a moment) and as you watch a golfer hit it into the water or go out of bounds or miss a putt, remember that is their job. Every day they are out at the range hitting balls, at the putting green working on speed control, at the gym trying to build muscle and stay in shape because the courses are getting longer. No one is perfect. Not even the pros! We see online instruction in the same light. It's a commitment, folks! This is not a game for those without a passion for it. The journey from starting as an online instructor to retiring after years of teaching online is a long one, but it's one that is full of growth and connection opportunities. Golfing, like online teaching, is an experience. It takes practice, planning, and persistence to be successful in either one and because of this we feel it's imperative to continually iterate your design, your instruction, and your administration practices in order to be successful.

It has probably become clear at this point that the elements of the PARS approach overlap and have a fluency to them that, when used together, creates a dynamic overarching experience. But at this point we feel it is important to remind readers that what we're talking about through this whole book is creating a user experience and through "good UX, you are trying to reduce the friction between the task someone wants to accomplish and the tool that they are using to complete that task" (Buley, 2013, p. 4). We hope that through reading the chapters in this text you feel better equipped to plan for and mitigate those friction points in your online writing courses. When working together with PARS, these user experience elements take an online course to a new level, further enhancing the experience for students. We know from an interview that Jon Kolko gave in 2010 that good design is "design that changes behavior for the better . . . [and takes] into account the context of the environment, of the human condition, the culture, and then attempt[s] to make the things you do" better (Laneri, 2010, para. 4).

If you've not gathered this already, design and strategy are everything in the success or failure of online writing courses and we cannot stress that you need to pay a lot of attention to these things as you put together distance education experiences for your students. Because as much as some hate to admit it, education is a product experience that students are purchasing and consuming and because of this we feel it's important to research and listen to the student consumers when creating online courses. Doing research about what your student users want and need is important. Some brief user research can go a long way to assisting the students in success in their distance education courses because "User research is about understanding users and their [the users'] needs, and user experience design is about designing a user's interactions with a product from moment to moment" (Buley, 2013, p. 5). Iterating your online courses, teaching and administration practices only creates better experiences for all involved. Listening to your instructors (as an administrator) or your students (as an instructor or administrator) will help you identify the touchpoints or the things that just aren't working as well as they should. Gaining this knowledge of issues related to the online course experience will guide you in your continual quest to be a better online program administrator or online instructor because you'll be able to take feedback and apply it to the next iteration of the program or course.

Getto and Beecher (2016) argue, "As more and more consumers look to digital products and services to perform everyday tasks, technical professionals of all stripes will need to support those experiences in myriad ways" (p. 157). With the growth of online education over the past ten years, colleges and universities across the country feel pressure to offer more courses for campus-based degrees via flexible learning formats, such as hybrid courses or fully online courses.

Jobs like Interaction Designer and Instructional Designer are finding their way into academic spaces to support faculty and students. The most recent distance education report noted that 29.7% of all students in higher education are taking at least one distance course. Of that 29.7%, students taking only distance courses make up 14.3%; students taking a combination of both traditional and online courses make up 15.4% (Allen & Seaman, 2017). Both of these trends—fully online degrees and degrees earned by a combination of traditional and online—will only grow and universities need to hire people who can help support this growth, or their students/users will attend schools who will support them.

In the fall of 2014, there were around six million students in the US who enrolled in online classes (Friedman, 2016), and the numbers continue to rise. User-centered design (UCD) "means understanding what your users need, how they think, and how they behave—and incorporating that understanding into every aspect of your process" (Garrett, n.d., para. 3). This process can be applied via three main principles of design: usability, accessibility, and sustainability. When creating an online course, educators must create a usable space for students to easily navigate, an accessible space to connect to from any country and from any hardware along with ADA compliance, and it must be sustainable in that the space can adapt and evolve as technologies and social contexts change. We know that more and more schools are adding or increasing online undergraduate and graduate degree programs and as they do, this will increase the demand on their campus-based programs to offer more online options. Already more undergraduate programs are being encouraged, if not required, to put introductory courses such as first-year writing online. We've seen this happen at our own institutions.

However, just because the need is there does not mean institutions should plunge headfirst into the distance education pool. We know from experience that user research is an important part of success in an online course and a degree program. And yet, many do not spend the time to do user research or user testing and the like. Users/students become an afterthought and user feedback is only gathered at the end of the course or upon degree completion. User experience research can be the answer, "UX learning opportunities have the potential to help academic organizations improve customer satisfaction and business strategy, as well as to help them better fulfill their mission" (Getto & Beecher, 2016, p. 158). We see the PARS approach as a way to apply a user-focused approach to your online courses so that your student users don't become an afterthought.

An easy way to ensure that your students remain the focus of your course design and instruction is to poll them for their opinions. For example, we do a debrief with our students all the time to get feedback on the subject, readings, methods, and structure of the course. This simple survey allows us to consider the voice of customer (VOC) and it's a quick and easy way to get some feedback on what is and is not working from your actual student users. We recommend you have a survey ready for your online classes as well that asks students what they are struggling with in terms of concepts, readings, accessibility, hardware, software, the CMS, and so on. You can send out this survey every week or pick a few key points in the semester to send it out. Mega companies such as Apple and Microsoft pour millions of dollars into getting user feedback before, during, and after launches of their products—why shouldn't an instructor do the same for their class?

Another idea we've honed after having worked with faculty and colleagues over the years on pedagogy, products, and processes, is an adapted five-day design sprint. Design sprints are typically used to solve problems. This five-day sprint can help to inform users of curriculum changes and course design developments. What you see in the example below is something Casey has used in the past based on Mark Di Sciullo's article "UX and Agile: How to Run a Product Design Sprint" (https://www.tandemseven.com/experience-design/ux-agile-run-product-design-sprint/). It's a great starting point and a good entry for people trying to understand UX concepts and methods and how to apply them to things in their daily lives. There are more robust sprints out there, so feel free to tailor each one to your needs. This is an example of how you might run it with your faculty or a group of online instructors to understand and solve some problems you might be having with an online writing course.

Day 1: Understand the Problem

Who are the users: students

Define the problem: they won't engage with discussion boards and respond

Terms: learning, feedback, discussion, interactive, feedback, writing

What will they find useful: ??

Related research: [sources here]

Competition: face-to-face

Notes:

Successful metrics: student engagement and number of posts increase? grades?

Testing: pick a class to pilot some new discussion board approaches

Day 2: Gain Insight

Create activities to generate insights and churn out many possible solutions to address the problem.

The team will explore as many ways of solving the problems as possible, regardless of how realistic, feasible, or viable they may or may not be.

Use games from *Gamestorming* (Gray, Brown & Macanufo, 2010) to get participants thinking about how to write and revise various feedback prompts in the discussion boards. Is it the posts? Is it the CMS? Is it the user interface?

Some outcomes might be:

- New feedback prompts
- New use of discussion boards
- Find a new CMS or deliverable for posts and asynchronous interactions between students

Day 3: Decisions

Come to a decision based on the results learned from Day 2. What are the causes? What are you going to do? Note that not every idea will be able to be explored and used in terms of fixing the problem (budget, tech, etc., reasons). Cull the suggestions down to the more viable solution.

- Game
  - ▷ Collect the most viable solutions based on Day 2's sprint
  - ▷ Identify conflicts
  - ▷ Eliminate solutions that cannot be pursued
  - ▷ List assumptions on agreed upon solution
  - ▷ Identify how to test solution

Day 4: Prototype

The goal for this day is to build a prototype you can test with users on your new feedback and discussion board model. You can use paper or generate easy to use mockups online via various software or even use Microsoft Word. The point is to do quick and easy prototypes of what you think might address the problems you identified and tested in the previous three days.

Day 5: Validate and Learn

The goal for this day is to get the design in front of existing and potential users (students) to identify what is working and what is not working and identify what requires more research.

Your target audience (students) is who you want to find your new space useful. The insights of the students will give you an understanding of if you are on the right track. You should know by the end of this day if you are on the right track and meeting the needs of your users/students while still delivering a knowledge making space advertised by your university and your curriculum.

For testing, observe and interview students as they interact with your new space. To test it compared to others, give students a chance to interact with a competitive space—maybe compare the old with the new. At the end of the day have a debrief with everyone involved with the sprint on the day's testing sessions.

Now, come up with an action plan developed from the sprint.

This example of a five-day sprint is an opportunity to get people together to work on a common problem and find solutions together. It is great for faculty to interact and share ideas to problems they have all experienced. It builds team-work and a better understanding of the goals of the program, the university mission, and the faculty.

Final Thoughts

We see UX playing a larger role in online writing instruction going forward and, as you use the PARS approach, we know you'll have a solid understanding of what it means to keep the users at the forefront of your processes and designs. We see this book as a conversation with fellow new/existing online writing instructors and administrators who need support *and* are willing to support one another. Far too often we attend conferences and hear amazing stories of pedagogical brilliance, courage, and vulnerability when it comes to teaching online. At one panel we would see people sharing trials while teaching and, in another panel, hear about successes. We thought we might cut through all of waves of research and anecdotes to create one text everyone can use. Because as we keep saying,

We are all online writing instructors!
And here's the t-shirt we made to prove it :)

References

Allen, I. E. & J. Seaman. (Feb. 2016). Report card: Tracking online education in the United States. *Babson Research Group*. Retrieved from http://onlinelearning survey.com/reports/onlinereportcard.pdf.

Baehr, C. & Cargile Cook, K. (2016). *The agile communicator: Principles and practices in technical communication*. Dubuque, IA: Kendall Hunt.

Buley, L. (2013). *The user experience team of one: A research and design survival guide*. Brooklyn, NY: Rosenfield.

Di Sciullo, M. (2015). UX and agile: How to run a product design sprint. Retrieved from https://www.tandemseven.com/experience-design/ux-agile-run-product -design-sprint/.

Friedman, J. (2017). The average online bachelor's student. Retrieved from https:// www.usnews.com/higher-education/online-education/articles/2017-04-04/us -news-data-the-average-online-bachelors-student.

Friedman, J. (2018). Study: More students are enrolling in online courses. Retrieved from https://www.usnews.com/higher-education/online-education/articles /2018-01-11/study-more-students-are-enrolling-in-online-courses.

Garrett, J. J. (n.d.) Quote. Retrieved from http://www.affordableusability.com/usabil ity/principles.html.

Getto, G. & Beecher, F. (2016). Toward a model of UX education: Training UX designers within the academy. *IEEE Transactions on Professional Communication, 59*(2), 153–164.

Gray, D., Brown, S., Macanufo, J. (2010). *Gamestorming: A playbook for innovators, rulebreakers, and changemakers.* Sebastopol, CA: O'Reilly.

Hewett, B. (2015). *Reading to learn and writing to teach: Literacy strategies for online writing instruction.* Boston, MA: Bedford St. Martin's.

Laneri, R. (2010). Jon Kolko on design that changes human behavior. Forbes.com. Retrieved from https://www.forbes.com/2010/06/15/jon-kolko-designer -technology-future-design-10-frog.html#1b3381f42bf6.

Leijten, M., Van Waes, L., Schriver, K. & Hayes, J. (2014). Writing in the workplace: Constructing documents using multiple digital sources. *Journal of Writing Research, 5*(3), 285–337.

National Center for Education Statistics. (2016). Characteristics of postsecondary students. Retrieved from http://nces.ed.gov/programs/coe/indicator_csb.asp.

Olson, S. A. (2016, May). Higher learning across three generations. *Sky Magazine,* 129–137.

Smith, D. F. (2014). Who is the average online college student? Retrieved from https://edtechmagazine.com/higher/article/2014/05/who-average-online-college -student-infographic.

Williams, J. (2014, September 22). College of tomorrow: The changing demographics of the student body. *USA Today.* Retrieved from http://www.usnews.com/news /college-of-tomorrow/articles/2014/09/22/college-of-tomorrow-the-changing -demographics-of-the-student-body.

Afterword

Bill Hart-Davidson
MICHIGAN STATE UNIVERSITY

In their closing chapter of this book, Jessie and Casey offer a guiding framework for colleagues preparing to teach online in UXD, user experience design. Grounded in both the research on effective online learning and their own years of experience, this is very sound advice. In my own experience teaching online, I have found that the biggest obstacles stem from the radical shift to a much more low-bandwidth environment than both teachers and students are used to in face-to-face, in-person learning environments (see Hart-Davidson, 2014). What do I mean by low-bandwidth?

Well consider how much information passes easily among all the members of a group of learners, including the instructor, when everyone is together in the same room. Just with a glance, as a teacher, I can get a very reliable measure of how well everybody is doing, who is engaged and who is not, who might need my help with something, and who among the group is willing and able to help others. Now consider what that same kind of status check would require in most online teaching settings. How long would it take you to work all of that out as a teacher? And once you had that information, how quickly could you act on it?

In online learning environments, we simply must practice an approach like PARS in order to make up our own inability to be improvisational, to shift things on the fly, as instructors may be accustomed to doing in face-to-face classrooms.

If we do not, what suffers most is something that we often take for granted as a key ingredient of learning: the interactions that lead to meaningful engagement.

If I were to be so audacious as to suggest a tagline for this book and the project it represents to Jessie and Casey, I would suggest something like this: "Four Key Steps to Creating Meaningful Interaction in Digital Learning Spaces." Those four steps?

Prioritize (P)ersonal connection, ensure an (A)ccessible experience, model and reward (R)esponsiveness, and make (S)trategic use of the affordances of digital spaces. If you do those four things, something amazing can happen. You not only can overcome the potential shortcomings of digital spaces such as the lack of bandwidth, you can help produce experiences that exceed the learning potential of face-to-face interaction!

Wait, did I lose you on that one? How could I go from lamenting the loss of improvisational freedom in a traditional face-to-face classroom to claiming that online learning, done the PARS way, might actually exceed the capacity to foster learning of a face-to-face classroom? The answer is pretty simple. PARS works in both settings equally well. And when we attend to all four, we can see that face-to-face classrooms might be putting some of our students at a disadvantage in ways we fail to notice or act on.

Let's take the principle of accessibility. And let's ask ourselves to be a bit literal and rigorous in how we measure whether something is accessible or not. What if, for instance, we evaluated the success of a class discussion (a many-to-many conversation) by how many people were able to participate? It is often the case that in an f2f classroom, we see just a few people interacting when we do a many-to-many activity like large group discussion. And for folks who are out that day, the chance to participate is lost. In online spaces, we can extend the time to participate and we can offer some benefits to folks who might not feel comfortable speaking up, or who might need a few extra minutes to gather their thoughts, before contributing. We might allow folks whose first language is not the language of instruction to enter the dialogue more easily. And I'm sure you can think of a few other affordances of digital spaces that could he used, strategically, to maximize access.

The key, once again, is to imagine that an important part of your work as an instructor—no matter if you are teaching online or in a traditional f2f classroom—is to be creating the conditions for certain kinds of interactions to happen. When I work with new teachers, I find this is not always top of mind. And it's understandable. We worry a lot about content and our mastery of that. But I want to emphasize here that PARS can help you think more carefully about not just the *topics* but the *structure* of interactions that will enable learning in your classrooms, regardless of where you teach.

And it is especially important to think about the interactions that students have with each other. More than any other thing, students' ability to interact with other learners is the thing at most risk in an online curriculum. To illustrate just how important that kind of peer interaction can be, I like to ask folks to consider a specific kind of face-to-face learning space meant to ensure maximum access to peer inter-action, often informal, that is critical to learning. I'm talking about a dance studio!

What are the key features of a dance studio? It is typically a large and open space, allowing multiple learners to practice together, ensuring unobstructed line-of-sight among learners and the instructor, but also allowing learners to es-tablish personal space. In a dance studio, your most valuable learning resources are . . . other learners! We learn from them by watching as they attempt to do what we are also attempting. We learn, moreover, equally well from seeing what they do right and seeing how they struggle. We learn by adjusting our own efforts to match our more capable peers and we learn even more when we make explicit to peers who turn to us for help how they might improve. Can your online learning environment do that? How can you use the PARS framework to make sure you create learning spaces that can do that?

A dance studio has something on the walls that is important too. Mirrors. They allow for . . . reflection. The ability to see one's one work in the moment, and in the context of others' practice, so we can make adjustments. A studio is a place for reflective practice. Where a successful attempt can be noticed, recognized as a model for others to follow, celebrated and repeated. It is also a place where an unsuccessful attempt can be broken down, understood, and turned into a more deliberate plan for success the next time. Mirrors make the studio into a maxi-mally responsive space, where we can establish that it is okay to make a mistake as long as we are responsive to feedback about how to improve.

I want just about all the spaces in which I teach and learn to be like a dance studio: populated with fellow learners whom I can share experiences with while I calibrate my intentions and efforts. I want a space where I can safely practice, but with an assurance that someone nearby will respond if I need a correction. I want to help others learn, too, because this means I can use my experience to help solidify and make more routine something that I have begun to master. Alas, not every learning space we teach in online is a dance studio right out of the box. Even if the potential exists for online spaces to be transformative for some learners, it takes a deliberate effort on the part of those who teach to help realize this potential. That is what this book, if you put the ideas of PARS into practice, will help you do.

References

Hart-Davidson, B. (2014). Learning many-to-many: The best case for writing in digital environments. In S. D. Krause & C. Lowe (Eds.), *Invasion of the MOOCs: The prom-ises and perils of massive open online courses* (pp. 212–222). Anderson, SC: Parlor Press. Retrieved from http://www.parlorpress.com/invasion_of_the_moocs.